Advanced Android Programming: Harnessing the Power of Mobile Apps

Alexeyzz Kuznetsov

Alexeyzz Kuznetsov is a seasoned mobile application developer and software architect with over a decade of experience in Android development. Known for his in-depth knowledge and expertise in building scalable, high-performance mobile applications, Alexeyzz has worked with startups and global tech companies alike, leading projects that have reached millions of users worldwide. His passion for mobile technology and dedication to code quality have earned him recognition within the developer community, where he has spoken at numerous tech conferences and contributed to open-source projects focused on Android and mobile technology.

Throughout his career, Alexeyzz has focused on pushing the boundaries of mobile app capabilities, from integrating cutting-edge machine learning models to implementing complex UI designs that enhance user engagement. He is particularly passionate about empowering other developers to excel in Android development through hands-on, practical education. In **Advanced Android Programming: Harnessing the Power of Mobile Apps**, he distills years of experience into actionable insights, sharing advanced techniques and best practices that will help developers build robust, innovative Android applications.

When he's not coding, Alexeyzz enjoys exploring new technologies, contributing to the open-source community, and mentoring up-and-coming developers, helping them reach their full potential in the ever-evolving field of mobile development.

In today's digital world, mobile applications are an essential part of our lives, enabling us to connect, work, play, and access information with ease. **Advanced Android Programming: Harnessing the Power of Mobile Apps** is designed for developers who are ready to take their Android development skills to the next level, from mastering the core components of the platform to integrating advanced, innovative features that enhance user experience and application performance.

This book goes beyond basic Android programming, diving into sophisticated techniques, tools, and frameworks that will empower you to build robust, high-quality apps that stand out in a competitive market. Each chapter tackles a critical aspect of Android development, providing hands-on examples, best practices, and insights to help you grow as a developer and create impactful, modern applications.

Chapter 1: Android Architecture and Core Components

Gain a strong foundation in Android's architecture, covering key layers such as the Linux kernel, application framework, and runtime environment. This chapter explores essential components like Activities, Services, Broadcast Receivers, and Content Providers, setting you up for efficient, modular app development.

Chapter 2: Efficient UI Design with Jetpack Compose

Explore Jetpack Compose, the latest toolkit for building Android UIs with speed and flexibility. Learn to create dynamic, responsive interfaces and manage state in Compose, optimizing your app's user experience.

Chapter 3: Advanced Navigation and Deep Linking

Master the Android Navigation Component to manage complex app navigation flows, including nested navigation and deep linking. This chapter also addresses adaptive navigation strategies for foldable devices and multi-window applications.

Chapter 4: Data Management with Room, LiveData, and ViewModel

Implement robust data storage and management using the Room database, LiveData, and ViewModel, while adhering to best practices for offline data handling and seamless data flow within your app.

Chapter 5: Networking and API Integration with Retrofit and RESTful APIs

Understand how to efficiently handle networking tasks, API integration, and real-time data with Retrofit and RESTful services. Explore techniques for handling API responses, caching, and optimizing network calls for improved app performance.

Chapter 6: Dependency Injection with Dagger and Hilt

Learn the principles of dependency injection and implement it with Dagger and Hilt to build scalable, testable applications. This chapter covers scoping, multi-module setups, and advanced dependency management for complex projects.

Chapter 7: Working with Background Tasks: WorkManager and Coroutines

Dive into background processing with WorkManager and Coroutines, enabling you to manage long-running tasks and optimize app performance for battery-sensitive operations.

Chapter 8: Enhanced User Experience with Animations and Transitions

Create engaging user interfaces with animations, transitions, and MotionLayout. Learn to craft dynamic experiences that captivate users while maintaining smooth app performance.

Chapter 9: Security and Data Protection in Android Apps

Secure your applications by implementing data encryption, biometric authentication, and secure networking practices. This chapter provides a comprehensive look at protecting user data and complying with modern security standards.

Chapter 10: Location and Map-Based Features with Google Maps API

Integrate Google Maps and location services to add powerful geospatial features to your app. Explore advanced map functionalities such as real-time tracking, geofencing, and custom map styling.

Chapter 11: Integrating Machine Learning with ML Kit and TensorFlow Lite

Enhance your app with machine learning capabilities using ML Kit and TensorFlow Lite. This chapter guides you through implementing image recognition, text processing, and optimizing ML models for mobile performance.

Chapter 12: Testing, Debugging, and Performance Optimization

Ensure your app performs at its best with techniques for testing, debugging, and profiling. This final chapter covers unit testing, UI testing with Espresso, and tools for optimizing memory, CPU, and battery usage.

By the end of Advanced Android Programming: Harnessing the Power of Mobile Apps, you will be equipped with the knowledge and tools to create advanced, feature-rich Android applications that meet high performance, usability, and security standards. Whether you are looking to expand your skill set, tackle more challenging projects, or lead in Android development, this book will serve as a comprehensive guide on your journey.

Chapter 1: Android Architecture and Core Components

In this chapter, we will explore the foundational elements of Android architecture, providing you with a comprehensive understanding of how the Android operating system is structured and how its various components interact. We will delve into the different layers of Android, including the Linux kernel, libraries, Android Runtime (ART), and the application framework. By examining core components such as Activities, Services, Broadcast Receivers, and Content Providers, you will gain insights into their roles and lifecycle management within an app. This foundational knowledge will set the stage for building modular, efficient applications and preparing you for more advanced concepts throughout the book.

1.1 Understanding Android's Architectural Layers

Android is a versatile and powerful operating system primarily designed for mobile devices. Its architecture is structured into several distinct layers, each serving a specific purpose and working together to deliver a seamless user experience. Understanding these architectural layers is crucial for developers as it provides insight into how Android operates and how different components interact. This knowledge is foundational for effective app development, enabling developers to make informed decisions about design, optimization, and troubleshooting.

Overview of Android Architecture

Android's architecture can be broadly divided into four primary layers:

- Linux Kernel Layer
- Hardware Abstraction Layer (HAL)
- Android Runtime and Libraries
- Application Framework
- Application Layer

Let's explore each layer in detail:

1. Linux Kernel Layer

At the base of the Android architecture lies the Linux kernel, which provides the core services for the operating system. The Linux kernel is responsible for managing hardware resources and providing a level of abstraction that allows software to interact with hardware components without needing to understand the specifics of the underlying hardware.

Key features of the Linux kernel in Android include:

- **Device Drivers**: The kernel contains drivers for various hardware components like the camera, touchscreen, GPS, and Wi-Fi. These drivers facilitate communication between the hardware and higher-level software components.
- **Process Management**: The Linux kernel handles the creation, scheduling, and termination of processes, ensuring that apps can run concurrently and efficiently without interfering with one another.
- **Memory Management**: It manages the allocation and deallocation of memory for applications, optimizing memory usage and ensuring that each app operates within its allocated resources.
- **Security**: The Linux kernel includes security features like user permissions, which help isolate applications from each other and protect the integrity of the system.

2. Hardware Abstraction Layer (HAL)

The Hardware Abstraction Layer serves as an interface between the Android framework and the hardware components of the device. HAL allows Android to interact with the hardware in a consistent way, irrespective of the specific hardware implementations from different manufacturers.

Key aspects of HAL include:

- **Standardized Interfaces**: HAL provides standardized interfaces for different hardware components, enabling developers to write code that can run on various devices without needing to modify it for different hardware.
- **Modular Design**: HAL is designed to be modular, allowing developers to create specific implementations for various hardware types, such as cameras or sensors, without affecting the higher layers of the Android architecture.

By decoupling hardware drivers from the Android framework, HAL allows developers to focus on building apps rather than dealing with the intricacies of hardware communication.

3. Android Runtime and Libraries

Above the HAL, we find the Android Runtime (ART) and a set of core libraries that provide essential functionalities for applications. ART is the environment where Android applications run, and it replaces the older Dalvik runtime.

Key components include:

- **Android Runtime (ART):** ART is responsible for executing Android applications. It compiles applications into native code upon installation, allowing for improved performance and reduced memory consumption. ART also supports features like garbage collection, which helps manage memory by automatically reclaiming space that is no longer in use.
- **Core Libraries**: Android provides a rich set of libraries that developers can utilize to access features like data storage, networking, graphics rendering, and user interface components. These libraries include support for Java and Kotlin, making it easier to develop applications using these programming languages.

The combination of ART and core libraries provides a robust foundation for app development, allowing developers to leverage existing functionalities while focusing on their specific application logic.

4. Application Framework

The application framework sits atop the Android runtime and serves as the intermediary between the underlying system and the applications themselves. It provides higher-level services that facilitate application development by abstracting away lower-level details.

Key components of the application framework include:

- **Activity Manager**: This component manages the lifecycle of applications and activities, handling tasks such as launching new activities, pausing, and resuming existing ones. It ensures that applications respond to user interactions and system events appropriately.
- **Content Providers**: Content providers allow applications to share data with other applications in a secure and controlled manner. They provide a standard interface for accessing and manipulating data stored in different formats, such as databases or files.

- **Resource Manager**: The resource manager handles various resources, including layouts, strings, and images, enabling developers to access and manage these resources in a structured way.
- **Notification Manager**: This service is responsible for managing notifications that appear in the status bar, allowing applications to communicate important events or updates to users.

By providing these services, the application framework simplifies the development process, allowing developers to focus on building features and functionality without having to manage the complexities of the underlying system.

5. Application Layer

At the top of the architecture lies the application layer, where individual Android applications reside. Each application runs in its own process and is isolated from other applications, ensuring security and stability. Developers create apps using the APIs provided by the application framework, leveraging the services and libraries available to build rich, interactive experiences.

Key characteristics of the application layer include:

- **Activity and Fragment Classes**: Activities represent individual screens or user interfaces within an app, while fragments are reusable UI components that can be combined to create flexible layouts.
- **Intents**: Intents are messaging objects that facilitate communication between components, allowing activities to start other activities, services, or broadcast receivers.
- **User Interface Components**: The application layer includes various UI components like buttons, text fields, and lists, which developers can customize to create engaging user interfaces.

The application layer is where developers bring their ideas to life, utilizing the lower layers of the Android architecture to create compelling and functional mobile applications.

Understanding Android's architectural layers is essential for developers aiming to create efficient, high-quality applications. Each layer serves a specific purpose and interacts with the others to provide a cohesive environment for app development. From the Linux kernel, which manages hardware resources, to the application layer, where user-facing applications reside, each component plays a critical role in the overall functionality of the Android operating system.

By grasping these architectural concepts, developers can make informed decisions about their app design and implementation strategies. Whether it's optimizing performance, managing memory efficiently, or leveraging Android's extensive APIs, a solid understanding of Android's architectural layers will enable developers to build better applications that deliver exceptional user experiences.

1.2 Activity and Fragment Lifecycle Deep Dive

Understanding the lifecycle of Activities and Fragments is crucial for Android developers, as it directly impacts application behavior, user experience, and resource management. Both Activities and Fragments have well-defined lifecycles that dictate how they are created, started, paused, resumed, and destroyed. This deep dive will cover each lifecycle state, the corresponding callback methods, and best practices for managing these states effectively.

Activity Lifecycle

An Activity represents a single screen with a user interface in an Android application. The lifecycle of an Activity is managed by the Android system, which calls specific methods in response to user interactions and system events. Here's a breakdown of the Activity lifecycle:

onCreate(Bundle savedInstanceState)

- This is the first callback method called when an Activity is created. It is where you initialize your Activity, set the layout, and instantiate any necessary components (e.g., views, variables).
- **Best Practices**: Always perform non-UI initialization here, such as setting up data binding, initializing ViewModels, and retrieving saved instance state.

onStart()

- Called when the Activity becomes visible to the user. This is where you can start animations or begin refreshing UI elements.
- **Best Practices**: Use this method to initialize UI elements that are required when the Activity is visible but not yet interactive.

onResume()

- Invoked when the Activity starts interacting with the user. This is the stage where the Activity is in the foreground.
- **Best Practices**: Register any listeners or start any processes that require user interaction. This is also a good place to start animations or refresh data.

onPause()

- Called when the system is about to put the Activity into the background, either because another Activity is coming to the foreground or because the user has navigated away from it.
- **Best Practices**: Use this method to pause ongoing actions (like animations), save unsaved changes, and release system resources that are not needed when the Activity is not in focus.

onStop()

- Invoked when the Activity is no longer visible to the user. This might happen if another Activity is in the foreground or the user navigates away from the app.
- **Best Practices**: Release any resources that are not needed while the Activity is stopped, save data to persistent storage, and unregister listeners.

onRestart()

- This callback is called when an Activity is coming back to the foreground from the stopped state. It occurs before onStart().
- **Best Practices**: Use this method to re-initialize resources that were released in onStop() and prepare the UI for the user.

onDestroy()

- This is the final call before the Activity is destroyed. It can be called either because the Activity is finishing or the system is temporarily destroying the Activity due to configuration changes (e.g., rotation).
- **Best Practices**: Perform final cleanup here, such as releasing resources and saving persistent data.

Fragment Lifecycle

A Fragment is a modular section of an Activity that has its own lifecycle. Fragments can be added or removed from Activities dynamically and are used to create responsive UI designs. The Fragment lifecycle is closely related to the Activity lifecycle, but it has its own distinct methods.

onAttach(Context context)

- This is the first callback when a Fragment is attached to its parent Activity. It is a good place to access the Activity context and initialize any components that require the Activity.
- **Best Practices**: Avoid heavy computations in this method; instead, use it for light initialization.

onCreate(Bundle savedInstanceState)

- Called to do initial creation of the Fragment. This is similar to the Activity's onCreate() method but is focused on the Fragment's data.
- **Best Practices**: Initialize variables and set up non-UI resources.

onCreateView(LayoutInflater inflater, ViewGroup container, Bundle savedInstanceState)

- Called to create the Fragment's UI. You must inflate the layout and return the root view.
- **Best Practices**: Return a properly initialized View, and remember to handle any saved state.

onActivityCreated(Bundle savedInstanceState)

- This callback is called when the Activity's onCreate() method has returned. It is where you can interact with the Activity's UI.
- **Best Practices**: Use this method to access the Activity's ViewModel or other components that need to interact with the Activity.

onStart()

- Similar to the Activity lifecycle, this method is called when the Fragment becomes visible.
- **Best Practices**: Use this to start animations or other visual elements.

onResume()

- This is called when the Fragment is visible and active, allowing interaction with the user.
- **Best Practices**: Register listeners and start any processes that require user interaction.

onPause()

- Called when the Fragment is no longer in the foreground.
- **Best Practices**: Save state and unregister listeners or other resources that should not remain active when the Fragment is not visible.

onStop()

- Invoked when the Fragment is no longer visible.
- **Best Practices**: Release resources that are not needed when the Fragment is not visible.

onDestroyView()

- Called when the Fragment's UI is being destroyed. This is the ideal place to clean up resources related to the UI.
- **Best Practices**: Release references to views to avoid memory leaks.

onDestroy()

- Similar to the Activity lifecycle, this method is called when the Fragment is being destroyed.
- **Best Practices**: Perform cleanup operations.

onDetach()

- Called when the Fragment is detached from the Activity. This is the last method called in the Fragment lifecycle.
- **Best Practices**: Clean up any references to the Activity context to prevent memory leaks.

Lifecycle and Configuration Changes

Both Activities and Fragments must handle configuration changes (such as device rotation) carefully. When a configuration change occurs, the current Activity is destroyed and recreated. To retain the state of the UI, developers can use:

onSaveInstanceState(Bundle outState): Use this method to save the current state before the Activity or Fragment is destroyed. The saved state can be restored in onCreate() or onCreateView().

ViewModel: By using the ViewModel architecture component, you can retain data across configuration changes without losing it during Activity or Fragment recreation.

Understanding the lifecycle of Activities and Fragments is fundamental for developing responsive and resource-efficient Android applications. By recognizing the various states and their corresponding callback methods, developers can manage resources effectively, preserve user state, and provide a seamless experience across different activities and configuration changes.

By adhering to best practices for each lifecycle method, you can ensure that your applications not only perform well but also offer a consistent and engaging user experience.

1.3 Services, Broadcast Receivers, and Content Providers

In Android development, Services, Broadcast Receivers, and Content Providers are essential components that enable communication and data management within and across applications. Each serves a unique purpose and interacts with the Android system differently. Understanding how to use these components effectively is crucial for creating robust and feature-rich applications.

1.3.1 Services

Definition: A Service in Android is a component that performs long-running operations in the background without a user interface. Services are designed to run in the background, allowing applications to handle tasks such as downloading files, playing music, or performing network operations.

Types of Services:

Started Services: These services are initiated by calling startService(Intent) and run independently of the Activity. Once started, they continue to run until they are stopped explicitly using stopSelf() or stopService(Intent). For example, a music player that continues playing in the background even when the user navigates away from the app is implemented using a started service.

Bound Services: These services allow components (like Activities) to bind to them and interact with them through a client-server interface. A bound service remains active as long as another component is bound to it. Once all clients unbind, the service is destroyed. For example, a service that provides data to an Activity or Fragment via a Messenger or a Binder.

Lifecycle of a Service:

- **onCreate():** Called when the service is first created. Initialization happens here.
- **onStartCommand():** Called each time a client starts the service using startService(). It returns an integer that indicates how the system should handle the service if it is killed (e.g., START_STICKY, START_NOT_STICKY).
- **onBind():** Called when a client binds to the service using bindService(). This method returns an interface for the client to interact with the service.
- **onUnbind():** Called when all clients have unbound from the service.
- **onDestroy():** Called when the service is no longer needed. Cleanup should be done here.

Best Practices:

- Use Services for tasks that should run independently of the user interface.
- Handle background work efficiently, considering battery consumption and resource usage.
- Utilize foreground services for tasks that are noticeable to the user (e.g., playing music).

1.3.2 Broadcast Receivers

Definition: A Broadcast Receiver in Android is a component that listens for and responds to system-wide broadcast announcements. These broadcasts can originate from the system (e.g., battery low, connectivity changes) or from other applications.

Types of Broadcasts:

- **Normal Broadcasts**: These broadcasts are asynchronous and are sent to all registered receivers at once. They are not guaranteed to be delivered in order.
- **Ordered Broadcasts**: These broadcasts are sent to one receiver at a time, in the order they are declared. Each receiver has the opportunity to stop the broadcast from continuing to other receivers.
- **Local Broadcasts**: These are broadcasts that can only be received within the same application, providing a way to communicate between components without exposing them to other applications.

Registering Broadcast Receivers:

- **Manifest Declaration**: Broadcast receivers can be declared in the AndroidManifest.xml file to listen for specific system events (e.g., BOOT_COMPLETED, CONNECTIVITY_CHANGE).
- **Runtime Registration**: Receivers can also be registered at runtime in an Activity or Service by calling registerReceiver() and unregistered with unregisterReceiver().

Lifecycle:

- When a broadcast is received, the system calls the onReceive(Context context, Intent intent) method of the registered BroadcastReceiver.
- The receiver executes its code and is terminated immediately after the method completes. This means that heavy operations should be offloaded to a Service to prevent blocking the UI thread.

Best Practices:

- Use local broadcasts for communication within the same app to avoid performance overhead.
- Be cautious with manifest-declared receivers, as they can consume resources even when the app is not running.
- Always unregister receivers registered at runtime to prevent memory leaks.

1.3.3 Content Providers

Definition: Content Providers are components that allow applications to manage and share structured data across different applications. They encapsulate the data and provide a standard interface for accessing it, making it easier to interact with databases or other data sources.

Use Cases:

- Sharing data between different applications, such as contacts, media files, or custom app data.
- Managing app data using SQLite databases, files, or remote servers.

Key Components:

- **URI**: Content Providers use Uniform Resource Identifiers (URIs) to identify the data they manage. This allows clients to access data in a consistent manner.
- **CRUD Operations**: Content Providers implement methods to handle Create, Read, Update, and Delete (CRUD) operations. The main methods include:
- **insert(Uri uri, ContentValues values)**: Inserts a new row of data.
- **query(Uri uri, String[] projection, String selection, String[] selectionArgs, String sortOrder)**: Retrieves data based on specified criteria.
- **update(Uri uri, ContentValues values, String selection, String[] selectionArgs)**: Updates existing data.
- **delete(Uri uri, String selection, String[] selectionArgs)**: Deletes data.

Lifecycle:

Content Providers do not have a lifecycle in the same sense as Activities or Services. However, they do respond to requests from clients. The onCreate() method is called when the Content Provider is created for the first time, where you can initialize any necessary resources.

Best Practices:

- Use Content Providers to encapsulate and manage data, providing a unified interface for accessing and manipulating it.
- Implement proper permissions to restrict access to sensitive data, ensuring that only authorized applications can interact with the Content Provider.
- Optimize queries to ensure efficient data retrieval and minimize performance overhead.

Services, Broadcast Receivers, and Content Providers are foundational components of the Android architecture that enable communication, background processing, and data management. Understanding how to implement and use these components effectively allows developers to create feature-rich applications that provide seamless user experiences.

Services facilitate long-running operations in the background, ensuring the user interface remains responsive.

Broadcast Receivers allow applications to listen for system-wide announcements, enabling them to react to changes or events occurring within the system or other applications.

Content Providers manage and share structured data across applications, allowing developers to encapsulate data access and provide a standardized interface.

By mastering these components, you can enhance your Android applications' functionality, responsiveness, and user engagement.

Chapter 2: Efficient UI Design with Jetpack Compose

In this chapter, we will dive into Jetpack Compose, Google's modern toolkit for building native Android UIs in a declarative manner. You'll learn how to create intuitive, responsive user interfaces that leverage composable functions, allowing for a more streamlined and flexible development process. We'll cover the fundamentals of building layouts, managing state, and handling user interactions, showcasing the advantages of using Jetpack Compose over traditional XML-based approaches. Additionally, we'll explore the rich ecosystem of Material Design components and animations available within Compose, equipping you with the skills to enhance user experience while ensuring that your applications are both visually appealing and performant. By the end of this chapter, you will be ready to harness the full potential of Jetpack Compose to build dynamic, engaging UIs for your Android applications.

2.1 Building and Structuring Composable Functions

Jetpack Compose, Android's modern toolkit for building native user interfaces, revolutionizes the way developers create UI components in Android applications. At the core of Compose is the concept of composable functions, which allow you to define and manage UI components declaratively. This section will explore how to build and structure composable functions effectively, focusing on best practices, compositional principles, and practical examples.

Understanding Composable Functions

A composable function is a special type of function annotated with @Composable, indicating that it can be used to define UI elements. These functions can take parameters and return UI elements, enabling developers to create reusable and maintainable code.

Basic Structure of a Composable Function:

```
@Composable
fun Greeting(name: String) {
    Text(text = "Hello, $name!")
}
```

In this example, the Greeting function takes a name parameter and displays a Text element greeting the user.

Key Principles of Composable Functions

Declarative UI: Compose uses a declarative approach, allowing developers to describe the UI in terms of what it should look like rather than how to achieve it. This means you define the state of your UI, and Compose takes care of rendering it.

Stateless vs. Stateful Composables:

- **Stateless Composables**: These functions do not maintain any internal state and rely entirely on parameters. They are easier to test and reuse.
- **Stateful Composables**: These manage their internal state using state management techniques like remember and mutableStateOf. Stateful composables can react to changes in state and update the UI accordingly.
- **Composition**: Composable functions can call other composable functions, enabling a hierarchical structure. This allows for building complex UIs from smaller, reusable components.

Recomposition: Compose automatically manages UI updates based on state changes. When state changes, Compose intelligently recomposes only the parts of the UI that depend on that state, optimizing performance.

Structuring Composable Functions

When building composable functions, maintaining a clean and organized structure is crucial for readability and maintainability. Here are some best practices for structuring your composables:

Single Responsibility Principle:

Each composable function should focus on a single task or UI element. This makes your code easier to read and understand.

```
@Composable
fun UserProfile(name: String, age: Int) {
    Column {
        UserName(name)
        UserAge(age)
```

```kotlin
    }
}

@Composable
fun UserName(name: String) {
    Text(text = "Name: $name")
}

@Composable
fun UserAge(age: Int) {
    Text(text = "Age: $age")
}
```
Parameterization:

Pass parameters to your composable functions to customize their behavior. This enhances reusability and flexibility.
kotlin
Copy code
```kotlin
@Composable
fun ButtonWithText(onClick: () -> Unit, text: String) {
    Button(onClick = onClick) {
        Text(text = text)
    }
}
```

Theming and Styling:

Use MaterialTheme and other styling functions to maintain a consistent look and feel across your application. Centralize your styling by defining reusable themes and styles.

```kotlin
@Composable
fun ThemedButton(onClick: () -> Unit, text: String) {
    Button(onClick = onClick, colors = ButtonDefaults.buttonColors(backgroundColor = MaterialTheme.colors.primary)) {
        Text(text = text, color = Color.White)
    }
}
```

State Management:

Use the remember and mutableStateOf functions to manage the state in your composable functions effectively. This allows you to maintain local state without relying on external data sources.

```
@Composable
fun Counter() {
    var count by remember { mutableStateOf(0) }

    Column {
        Text(text = "Count: $count")
        Button(onClick = { count++ }) {
            Text(text = "Increment")
        }
    }
}
```

Handling Side Effects:

Use LaunchedEffect and rememberCoroutineScope to handle side effects like launching coroutines or performing asynchronous operations within your composable functions.

```
@Composable
fun DataLoader() {
    var data by remember { mutableStateOf<String?>(null) }
    val coroutineScope = rememberCoroutineScope()

    LaunchedEffect(Unit) {
        data = fetchDataFromApi()
    }

    Text(text = data ?: "Loading...")
}
```

Example: Building a Simple UI with Composables

Let's look at a complete example of building a simple user profile UI using composable functions.

```
@Composable
fun UserProfileScreen(user: User) {
```

```
Column(modifier = Modifier.padding(16.dp)) {
    ProfilePicture(user.pictureUrl)
    UserName(user.name)
    UserBio(user.bio)
    ActionButtons(user.isFollowing)
  }
}

@Composable
fun ProfilePicture(url: String) {
    Image(painter = rememberImagePainter(url), contentDescription = "Profile Picture",
modifier = Modifier.size(100.dp))
}

@Composable
fun UserName(name: String) {
    Text(text = name, style = MaterialTheme.typography.h5)
}

@Composable
fun UserBio(bio: String) {
    Text(text = bio, style = MaterialTheme.typography.body2)
}

@Composable
fun ActionButtons(isFollowing: Boolean) {
    Row {
      Button(onClick = { /* Follow/Unfollow logic */ }) {
          Text(text = if (isFollowing) "Unfollow" else "Follow")
      }
      Spacer(modifier = Modifier.width(8.dp))
      Button(onClick = { /* Message logic */ }) {
          Text(text = "Message")
      }
    }
}
```

In this example, the UserProfileScreen composable organizes the UI into distinct components: ProfilePicture, UserName, UserBio, and ActionButtons. Each of these components is responsible for rendering a specific part of the user profile, adhering to the Single Responsibility Principle.

Building and structuring composable functions in Jetpack Compose is essential for creating efficient, maintainable, and scalable UIs. By following best practices such as keeping functions focused, managing state effectively, and composing smaller components, developers can harness the full potential of Jetpack Compose.

As you create more complex UIs, remember to leverage Compose's powerful features, including state management and recomposition, to deliver seamless and responsive user experiences. Understanding and mastering composable functions will empower you to build modern Android applications that are both functional and visually appealing.

2.2 Managing State in Jetpack Compose

State management is a critical aspect of building user interfaces in Jetpack Compose. Since Compose is built on a declarative paradigm, understanding how to manage state effectively is essential for ensuring that your UI responds correctly to user interactions and changes in data. This section will explore the various approaches to managing state in Jetpack Compose, including concepts like mutable state, state hoisting, and using state with ViewModels.

Understanding State in Jetpack Compose

In Jetpack Compose, the UI is rendered based on the current state. Whenever the state changes, the UI is recomposed to reflect those changes. This mechanism allows for a more intuitive and responsive user interface compared to traditional imperative UI frameworks.

Key Concepts:

- **State**: Represents the current data or information that affects the UI. In Compose, state can be any data type, but it must be managed in a way that informs Compose when it needs to update the UI.
- **Recomposition**: The process through which Compose updates the UI in response to state changes. It is efficient, meaning that only the parts of the UI that depend on the changed state are redrawn.

Managing State: Techniques and Tools

Using remember and mutableStateOf:

The remember function allows you to retain state across recompositions. It only remembers the value as long as the composable is in the composition. This is particularly useful for storing UI-related state.

mutableStateOf creates a mutable state holder that notifies Compose when its value changes, triggering recomposition.

Example:

```
@Composable
fun Counter() {
    // Remember the state across recompositions
    var count by remember { mutableStateOf(0) }

    Column(horizontalAlignment = Alignment.CenterHorizontally) {
        Text(text = "Count: $count")
        Button(onClick = { count++ }) {
            Text(text = "Increment")
        }
    }
}
```

State Hoisting:

State hoisting is a pattern that allows you to pass state and event handlers down to composables. Instead of a composable managing its own state, it receives state as a parameter, making it more reusable and testable.

Example:

```
@Composable
fun Counter( count: Int, onIncrement: () -> Unit) {
    Column(horizontalAlignment = Alignment.CenterHorizontally) {
        Text(text = "Count: $count")
        Button(onClick = onIncrement) {
            Text(text = "Increment")
        }
```

```
    }
}

@Composable
fun CounterScreen() {
    var count by remember { mutableStateOf(0) }

    Counter(count = count, onIncrement = { count++ })
}
```

In this example, the Counter composable takes count and onIncrement as parameters, allowing it to be used in different contexts with different states.

Using ViewModel for State Management:

ViewModels are part of Android's architecture components and are designed to hold and manage UI-related data in a lifecycle-conscious way. They survive configuration changes, making them ideal for storing state in Compose.

Example:

```
class CounterViewModel : ViewModel() {
    private val _count = mutableStateOf(0)
    val count: State<Int> get() = _count

    fun increment() {
        _count.value++
    }
}

@Composable
fun CounterScreen(viewModel: CounterViewModel = viewModel()) {
    Column(horizontalAlignment = Alignment.CenterHorizontally) {
        Text(text = "Count: ${viewModel.count.value}")
        Button(onClick = { viewModel.increment() }) {
            Text(text = "Increment")
        }
    }
}
```

In this example, CounterViewModel holds the state and provides methods to modify it. The UI reflects the current state stored in the ViewModel, and it survives configuration changes like screen rotations.

Using derivedStateOf:

The derivedStateOf function allows you to create a state that is derived from other state values. It helps avoid unnecessary recompositions when a value depends on multiple states.

Example:

```
@Composable
fun UserGreeting(name: String) {
    // Deriving a state that depends on the `name`
    val greeting by remember { derivedStateOf { "Hello, $name!" } }
    Text(text = greeting)
}
```

Using Side Effects with State:

Sometimes, you need to perform actions based on state changes. You can use LaunchedEffect or SideEffect for such purposes.

Example:

```
@Composable
fun DataLoader(data: String) {
    LaunchedEffect(data) {
        // Perform side effect based on data change
        println("Data loaded: $data")
    }
    Text(text = data)
}
```

Best Practices for State Management

Keep State Close to Where It Is Used:

Store state as close as possible to the UI that uses it. This minimizes complexity and makes it easier to understand how state changes affect the UI.

Avoid Mutating State Directly:

Instead of mutating state directly, use the provided mechanisms (mutableStateOf, ViewModel) to ensure that Compose is notified of changes.

Leverage ViewModels for Long-Lived State:

Use ViewModels to handle UI state that needs to survive configuration changes, ensuring a smooth user experience.

Minimize Recomposition:

Structure your composables to minimize the impact of state changes on the overall UI. Use derived states when necessary to avoid redundant recompositions.

Testing State Management:

Make your composables more testable by hoisting state and passing it as parameters. This practice makes it easier to write unit tests for your composable functions.

Managing state in Jetpack Compose is fundamental for creating responsive and dynamic user interfaces. By utilizing techniques like remember, state hoisting, and ViewModels, developers can ensure that their applications respond correctly to user interactions and data changes.

As you work with Compose, keep in mind the best practices for state management, ensuring that your UI is efficient, maintainable, and user-friendly. Understanding how to manage state effectively will empower you to build modern, robust Android applications that provide a seamless experience for users.

2.3 Animations and Interactivity in Compose

Animations and interactivity are essential components of a modern user interface. They not only enhance user experience but also make applications feel more responsive and engaging. Jetpack Compose simplifies the process of implementing animations and interactive elements, enabling developers to create rich, dynamic user experiences with ease. This section will cover the basics of animations and interactivity in Jetpack Compose, including different types of animations, handling gestures, and best practices for creating fluid interactions.

Understanding Animations in Jetpack Compose

Jetpack Compose provides a powerful framework for creating animations that can be easily integrated into your UI. The core principles of animations in Compose revolve around managing the state that drives the animation, defining transitions, and creating animated values.

Types of Animations:

Transition Animations:

Transition animations are used to animate changes between different UI states. You define the initial and final states, and Compose handles the animation for you.

Example:

```
@Composable
fun AnimatedVisibilityExample(visible: Boolean) {
    val transition = updateTransition(targetState = visible, label = "VisibilityTransition")

    val alpha by transition.animateFloat(
        transitionSpec = { tween(durationMillis = 300) },
        label = "AlphaAnimation"
    ) { state ->
        if (state) 1f else 0f
    }

    Box(modifier = Modifier.fillMaxSize().graphicsLayer(alpha = alpha)) {
        Text(text = "Hello, World!", modifier = Modifier.align(Alignment.Center))
    }
}
```

Animated Values:

Animated values allow you to animate properties such as size, position, color, or any other property. Compose provides built-in functions like animateDpAsState, animateColorAsState, and more.

Example:

```
@Composable
fun AnimatedSizeExample() {
    var expanded by remember { mutableStateOf(false) }
    val size by animateDpAsState(if (expanded) 200.dp else 100.dp)

    Box(
        modifier = Modifier
            .size(size)
            .background(Color.Blue)
            .clickable { expanded = !expanded }
    )
}
```

Keyframe Animations:

Keyframe animations allow you to define a sequence of values for a property at specific points in time. This type of animation provides more control over how the animation progresses.

Example:

```
@Composable
fun KeyframeAnimationExample() {
    val transition = rememberInfiniteTransition()
    val offsetX by transition.animateFloat(
        initialValue = 0f,
        targetValue = 100f,
        animationSpec = infiniteRepeatable(
            animation = keyframes {
                durationMillis = 1000
                0f at 0 with FastOutSlowInEasing // Start
                50f at 500 // Midpoint
                100f at 1000 with FastOutSlowInEasing // End
            }
```

```
        )
    )

    Box(
        modifier = Modifier
            .offset(x = offsetX.dp)
            .size(50.dp)
            .background(Color.Red)
    )
}
```

Handling Interactivity in Jetpack Compose

Interactivity is a core aspect of mobile applications, and Jetpack Compose provides a rich set of tools for handling user gestures and events.

Handling Clicks:

The Modifier.clickable is used to make a composable respond to click events. You can specify click listeners to perform actions when the composable is tapped.

Example:

```
@Composable
fun ClickableButton() {
    var clicked by remember { mutableStateOf(false) }

    Button(onClick = { clicked = !clicked }) {
        Text(if (clicked) "Clicked!" else "Click Me!")
    }
}
```

Gestures:

Compose provides various gesture detectors such as Modifier.pointerInput, which allows you to handle complex gestures like dragging, scaling, or swiping.

Example:

```
@Composable
```

```
fun DraggableBox() {
    var offsetX by remember { mutableStateOf(0f) }
    var offsetY by remember { mutableStateOf(0f) }

    Box(
        modifier = Modifier
            .offset(x = offsetX.dp, y = offsetY.dp)
            .size(100.dp)
            .background(Color.Green)
            .pointerInput(Unit) {
                detectDragGestures { change, dragAmount ->
                    offsetX += dragAmount.x
                    offsetY += dragAmount.y
                    change.consume()
                }
            }
    )
}
```

Using LaunchedEffect for Side Effects:

Use LaunchedEffect to perform side effects in response to state changes, such as triggering animations or fetching data based on user interactions.

Example:

```
@Composable
fun AnimatedGreeting(name: String) {
    var visible by remember { mutableStateOf(false) }

    LaunchedEffect(name) {
        visible = true
    }

    if (visible) {
        Text(text = "Hello, $name!", Modifier.animateContentSize())
    }
}
```

Best Practices for Animations and Interactivity

Keep Animations Subtle:

While animations can enhance user experience, it's essential to keep them subtle and not overly distracting. Use animations to provide feedback, guide user interactions, or indicate transitions between states.

Use Easing Functions:

Compose provides various easing functions (e.g., FastOutSlowInEasing, LinearEasing) to control the pacing of your animations. Choose easing functions that suit the nature of the animation and enhance the user experience.

Avoid Overusing Animations:

Use animations judiciously. Overuse can lead to a cluttered UI and may detract from the overall user experience. Focus on critical interactions that benefit from animation.

Test on Different Devices:

Performance can vary across devices. Test your animations on various screen sizes and performance levels to ensure a smooth user experience.

Document Your Animation Logic:

Keep your animation logic clear and well-documented, especially if it involves complex transitions or multiple states. This will help you and your team understand and maintain the animation code in the future.

Animations and interactivity are integral to creating engaging and responsive user interfaces in Jetpack Compose. By leveraging the framework's powerful animation capabilities and intuitive gesture handling, developers can craft applications that not only look good but also feel great to use.

Understanding the types of animations, how to manage state effectively, and how to handle user interactions will enable you to create fluid, dynamic experiences that captivate your users. As you continue to explore Jetpack Compose, keep in mind the best practices for animations and interactivity to ensure that your applications are both enjoyable and performant.

Chapter 3: Advanced Navigation and Deep Linking

In this chapter, we will explore the complexities of navigation in Android applications, focusing on the Android Navigation Component to facilitate seamless user experiences. You will learn how to create and manage navigation graphs, implement nested navigation for modular app structures, and handle transitions between different screens efficiently. We will also cover deep linking, enabling users to navigate directly to specific content within your app via URLs, which is crucial for enhancing user engagement and retention. By understanding adaptive navigation patterns for various device configurations, including foldable and multi-window setups, you'll gain the skills necessary to build sophisticated navigation flows that keep users oriented and engaged throughout their journey in your app. By the end of this chapter, you will be equipped to implement advanced navigation techniques and optimize user pathways for a more intuitive app experience.

3.1 Setting Up Navigation Components for Complex Flows

Navigating between different screens and managing complex flows is a fundamental aspect of mobile app development. Jetpack Compose offers a flexible and powerful navigation component that simplifies the process of setting up navigation in your applications. This section will cover how to use the Navigation component in Jetpack Compose to manage complex navigation flows, including nested navigation, argument passing, and deep linking.

Understanding Navigation in Jetpack Compose

In Jetpack Compose, navigation is handled by the Navigation library, which allows you to define navigation graphs. A navigation graph is a structure that represents all the destinations (screens) in your app and how users can navigate between them. This graph is built using composable functions, making it intuitive to visualize and manage your app's navigation flow.

Key Concepts:

- **Destinations**: These are the screens in your app (e.g., HomeScreen, DetailsScreen) that users can navigate to.

- **Actions**: These are the operations that trigger navigation, such as button clicks or specific user interactions.
- **Arguments**: Data that can be passed between destinations, enabling screens to display dynamic content based on user interactions.

Setting Up Navigation in Jetpack Compose

- **Adding Dependencies**: To use Jetpack Compose Navigation, you need to add the necessary dependencies to your build.gradle file:

```
dependencies {
    implementation "androidx.navigation:navigation-compose:<version>"
}
```

Replace <version> with the latest version of the navigation library.

Creating the Navigation Graph: The navigation graph defines all the routes in your app. You can create a navigation graph using the NavHost composable.

Example:

```
@Composable
fun MyNavHost() {
    val navController = rememberNavController()
    NavHost(navController, startDestination = "home") {
        composable("home") { HomeScreen(navController) }
        composable("details/{itemId}") { backStackEntry ->
            val itemId = backStackEntry.arguments?.getString("itemId")
            DetailsScreen(navController, itemId)
        }
    }
}
```

In this example, we set up a simple navigation graph with two destinations: HomeScreen and DetailsScreen. The DetailsScreen takes an argument (itemId) that is passed from the HomeScreen.

Navigating Between Screens: To navigate between screens, you can use the navController.navigate function. This function allows you to specify the destination and any arguments to pass.

Example:

```
@Composable
fun HomeScreen(navController: NavController) {
    Button(onClick = { navController.navigate("details/${itemId}") }) {
        Text("Go to Details")
    }
}
```

In this example, when the button is clicked, it triggers navigation to the DetailsScreen while passing the itemId as an argument.

Handling Up Navigation: It's essential to manage the back stack correctly to provide a smooth user experience. You can use the navController.popBackStack() method to handle back navigation, which allows users to return to the previous screen.

Example:

```
@Composable
fun DetailsScreen(navController: NavController, itemId: String?) {
    Column {
        Text("Details for Item: $itemId")
        Button(onClick = { navController.popBackStack() }) {
            Text("Back")
        }
    }
}
```

Managing Nested Navigation

For complex applications, you might need nested navigation graphs to manage related screens efficiently. This allows for better organization of your navigation structure.

Example:

```
@Composable
fun MainNavHost() {
    val navController = rememberNavController()
    NavHost(navController, startDestination = "home") {
```

```
    composable("home") { HomeScreen(navController) }
    navigation(startDestination = "settings", route = "settings_graph") {
        composable("settings") { SettingsScreen(navController) }
        composable("settings/details") { SettingsDetailsScreen(navController) }
    }
  }
}
```

In this example, the settings_graph encapsulates related settings screens, allowing you to manage them under a single navigation route.

Passing Arguments Between Screens

Passing data between screens is essential for dynamic content rendering. Jetpack Compose makes this straightforward with navigation arguments.

Example:

```
@Composable
fun DetailsScreen(navController: NavController, itemId: String?) {
    // Use itemId to fetch or display specific details
}
```

When navigating to the DetailsScreen, ensure you construct the route correctly to include the necessary arguments.

Deep Linking

Deep linking allows users to navigate directly to a specific screen in your app from an external source (e.g., a web link). Jetpack Compose supports deep links through the navigation component.

Example: To enable deep linking, you can define a route with a specific pattern in your navigation graph:

```
composable("details/{itemId}", deepLinks = listOf(navDeepLink { uriPattern =
"myapp://details/{itemId}" })) {
    backStackEntry ->
    val itemId = backStackEntry.arguments?.getString("itemId")
    DetailsScreen(navController, itemId)
```

```
}
```

In this case, the app can be opened directly to a specific DetailsScreen using the deep link.

Best Practices for Navigation in Compose

Keep Navigation Simple: Avoid overly complex navigation flows. Aim for simplicity to make it easier for users to navigate your app.

Use Clear and Descriptive Routes: Define clear and descriptive route names for your screens to enhance readability and maintainability.

Manage Back Stack Appropriately: Utilize the back stack effectively to provide a smooth user experience. Ensure that users can easily navigate back to previous screens.

Leverage Nested Navigation: Use nested navigation graphs to organize related screens and avoid clutter in your main navigation graph.

Implement Deep Links: Support deep links to enhance user engagement and allow users to access specific content directly.

Setting up navigation components in Jetpack Compose allows you to manage complex navigation flows efficiently. By leveraging the navigation graph, passing arguments, and supporting deep linking, you can create intuitive and user-friendly applications.

Understanding the navigation component in Compose will enable you to design seamless user experiences that feel natural and responsive. As you build more complex applications, keep in mind the best practices for navigation to ensure your app remains easy to navigate and understand.

3.2 Implementing Deep Links and App Links

Deep linking is a powerful feature that allows your mobile application to respond to URLs, enabling users to navigate directly to specific content within your app from external sources like websites, email, or other apps. In Jetpack Compose, implementing deep links and app links can enhance the user experience by providing seamless access to specific content. This section will cover the concepts of deep links and app links, how to implement them in your Jetpack Compose application, and best practices for effective usage.

Understanding Deep Links and App Links

Deep Links: A deep link is a URL that points to a specific location within a mobile app. When a user clicks on a deep link, the app opens to a specified screen, allowing them to view specific content without navigating through the app's hierarchy.

App Links: App links are a type of deep link that can open an app directly when a user clicks on a link in a web browser or another app. They provide a seamless experience by allowing URLs to open an app instead of navigating to a website.

Setting Up Deep Links in Jetpack Compose

To implement deep links in Jetpack Compose, follow these steps:

Define the Deep Link in the Navigation Graph: You need to define deep links within your navigation graph using the deepLinks parameter. This allows the navigation component to handle incoming intents that match your specified URI patterns.

Example:

```
@Composable
fun MyNavHost() {
    val navController = rememberNavController()
    NavHost(navController, startDestination = "home") {
        composable("home") { HomeScreen(navController) }

        composable(
            "details/{itemId}",
            deepLinks = listOf(navDeepLink { uriPattern = "myapp://details/{itemId}" })
        ) { backStackEntry ->
            val itemId = backStackEntry.arguments?.getString("itemId")
            DetailsScreen(navController, itemId)
        }
    }
}
```

In this example, we define a deep link for the DetailsScreen. The deep link can be activated with a URL like myapp://details/123, where 123 is the itemId to be displayed.

Declare the Intent Filter in the AndroidManifest.xml: To handle deep links, you need to declare an <intent-filter> in the AndroidManifest.xml file for the corresponding activity. This filter tells the system which URLs your app can respond to.

Example:

```
<activity
    android:name=".MainActivity">
    <intent-filter>
        <action android:name="android.intent.action.VIEW" />
        <category android:name="android.intent.category.DEFAULT" />
        <category android:name="android.intent.category.BROWSABLE" />
        <data android:scheme="myapp" android:host="details" android:pathPattern="/.*" />
    </intent-filter>
</activity>
```

In this example, the intent-filter allows the app to respond to URLs that start with myapp://details/.

Handling Incoming Intents: Inside your main activity, you may want to handle incoming intents and direct them to the appropriate screen based on the URL.

Example:

```
class MainActivity : ComponentActivity() {
    override fun onCreate(savedInstanceState: Bundle?) {
        super.onCreate(savedInstanceState)
        setContent {
            MyNavHost()
        }
        handleDeepLink(intent)
    }

    private fun handleDeepLink(intent: Intent?) {
        intent?.data?.let { uri ->
            // Here you can parse the URI and navigate to the corresponding screen
            val navController = rememberNavController()
            when (uri.path) {
                "/details" -> {
                    val itemId = uri.lastPathSegment
```

```
                navController.navigate("details/$itemId")
            }
        }
    }
  }
}
```

In this example, we check the incoming intent for a URI and navigate to the appropriate destination based on the path.

Implementing App Links

App links are similar to deep links but provide a more seamless experience, as they can open the app directly from a browser. To implement app links, you need to follow similar steps with a few adjustments.

Define App Links in the AndroidManifest.xml: You can define app links using the same <intent-filter> mechanism as deep links. However, you may want to include additional attributes to specify that it is an app link.

Example:

```
<activity
   android:name=".MainActivity">
   <intent-filter android:autoVerify="true">
     <action android:name="android.intent.action.VIEW" />
     <category android:name="android.intent.category.DEFAULT" />
     <category android:name="android.intent.category.BROWSABLE" />
     <data android:scheme="https" android:host="www.mywebsite.com" />
   </intent-filter>
</activity>
```

Here, we specify an https scheme and a www.mywebsite.com host. The android:autoVerify="true" attribute allows the system to verify that your app can handle the link.

Set Up Digital Asset Links: To ensure that your app is correctly associated with your website, create a Digital Asset Links file. This file informs Android that your app is the owner of the domain. You need to host a JSON file on your website with the following content:

```
[
  {
    "relation": ["delegate_permission/common.handle_all_urls"],
    "target": {
      "namespace": "android_app",
      "package_name": "com.example.myapp",
      "sha256_cert_fingerprints": [
        "YOUR_APP_SHA256_CERT_FINGERPRINT"
      ]
    }
  }
]
```

Replace YOUR_APP_SHA256_CERT_FINGERPRINT with the actual SHA-256 fingerprint of your app's signing certificate.

Testing App Links: Once everything is set up, test your app links by clicking links on your website or using tools like the ADB command:

adb shell am start -W -a android.intent.action.VIEW -d "https://www.mywebsite.com/details/123" com.example.myapp

This command simulates a click on a web link, and your app should open to the specified screen.

Best Practices for Deep Links and App Links

Use Clear and Consistent URL Patterns: Design your URL patterns to be clear and consistent. This makes it easier for users to understand where the link will take them and improves the maintainability of your code.

Implement Fallbacks: Always implement fallback mechanisms for users who may not have your app installed. Ensure that your links lead to a meaningful experience on the web if the app cannot be opened.

Test Thoroughly: Test your deep links and app links thoroughly to ensure they work as expected across various scenarios, including when the app is closed, in the background, or already open.

Monitor Analytics: Use analytics tools to monitor how users are interacting with your deep links and app links. This data can help you optimize the experience and make informed decisions about future features.

Keep User Experience in Mind: Ensure that your deep linking experience feels seamless and intuitive. The transition between web links and app content should be smooth to avoid confusing users.

Implementing deep links and app links in your Jetpack Compose application allows you to enhance user engagement by providing direct access to specific content. By defining deep links in your navigation graph, setting up intent filters, and handling incoming links appropriately, you can create a seamless user experience.

Understanding and effectively using deep linking and app linking will empower you to create applications that are not only user-friendly but also highly functional and integrated with web content. As you continue to develop your app, keep in mind the best practices for managing deep links to maximize their impact.

3.3 Handling Adaptive and Multi-Stack Navigation

In modern mobile applications, users expect a seamless experience as they navigate through different screens. Adaptive and multi-stack navigation strategies allow developers to create flexible and user-friendly interfaces that cater to diverse user needs and device configurations. This section will delve into the principles of adaptive navigation, explore multi-stack navigation patterns, and provide practical guidance on implementing these strategies using Jetpack Compose.

Understanding Adaptive Navigation

Adaptive Navigation refers to the ability of an application to adjust its navigation structure based on different contexts, such as screen size, device orientation, and user behavior. For example, on larger screens like tablets, you might want to display more information side-by-side instead of navigating to a new screen. Conversely, on smaller screens, a simpler, more linear navigation structure may be more appropriate.

Key Principles of Adaptive Navigation:

- **Context-Aware Design**: Design your navigation structure to adapt based on the context, such as device type (mobile, tablet) or user preferences.

- **Flexible Layouts**: Use responsive layouts that can rearrange content based on available space, providing a cohesive experience across devices.
- **Consistent User Experience**: Ensure that navigation remains intuitive and consistent, even as it adapts to different contexts.

Implementing Adaptive Navigation in Jetpack Compose

Using Box and Row for Adaptive Layouts: Jetpack Compose offers flexible layout composables like Box and Row that allow you to create adaptive UIs. By arranging components dynamically, you can cater to various screen sizes.

Example:

```
@Composable
fun AdaptiveScreen(isTablet: Boolean) {
    if (isTablet) {
        Row {
            // Show a list on the left and details on the right
            ItemList()
            ItemDetail()
        }
    } else {
        Column {
            ItemList()
            ItemDetail()
        }
    }
}
```

In this example, if the device is identified as a tablet, the layout uses a Row to display the item list and details side-by-side. On smaller screens, it uses a Column to stack them vertically.

Responsive Design with Constraints: Use the Modifier to adjust the size and arrangement of composables based on the screen size or orientation.

Example:

```
@Composable
fun ResponsiveLayout() {
```

```
val screenWidth = LocalConfiguration.current.screenWidthDp
if (screenWidth > 600) {
    // Show expanded layout for larger screens
    ExpandedLayout()
} else {
    // Show compact layout for smaller screens
    CompactLayout()
  }
}
```

Here, the app checks the screen width and applies different layouts based on the width, providing a more tailored experience for users.

Utilizing Navigation Destinations: You can define navigation destinations in your navigation graph that accommodate different devices. Consider creating separate routes for tablet and mobile views.

Example:

```
NavHost(navController, startDestination = "home") {
    composable("home") { HomeScreen(navController) }
    composable("tabletHome") { TabletHomeScreen(navController) }
}
```

This approach allows you to define distinct screens for different device types, enhancing user experience.

Understanding Multi-Stack Navigation

Multi-Stack Navigation refers to a pattern where multiple navigation stacks coexist within an application, allowing users to navigate independently between different flows. This pattern is especially useful in applications that feature distinct areas or functionalities that may require separate navigation paths.

Benefits of Multi-Stack Navigation:

- **Improved User Experience**: Users can switch between different parts of the app without losing their current place in each flow.
- **Enhanced Performance**: By isolating navigation stacks, the app can manage resources more efficiently, leading to better performance.

- **Separation of Concerns**: Each navigation stack can be tailored to specific tasks or features, reducing complexity.

Implementing Multi-Stack Navigation in Jetpack Compose

Using Nested Navigation Hosts: To implement multi-stack navigation, you can create nested NavHost components. Each NavHost can manage its own navigation stack, allowing independent navigation within different sections of the app.

Example:

```
@Composable
fun MainNavHost() {
    val navController = rememberNavController()
    NavHost(navController, startDestination = "home") {
        composable("home") { HomeScreen(navController) }
        navigation(startDestination = "settings", route = "settings_graph") {
            composable("settings") { SettingsScreen(navController) }
            composable("profile") { ProfileScreen(navController) }
        }
        navigation(startDestination = "shop", route = "shop_graph") {
            composable("shop") { ShopScreen(navController) }
            composable("cart") { CartScreen(navController) }
        }
    }
}
```

In this example, the app has separate navigation graphs for settings and shop-related features, allowing users to navigate independently within these areas.

Managing Back Stack with Multiple Navigation Hosts: Each navigation stack should maintain its own back stack. Use navController.popBackStack() to handle back navigation within the correct stack.

Example:

```
@Composable
fun SettingsScreen(navController: NavController) {
    Column {
        Text("Settings")
```

```
        Button(onClick = { navController.popBackStack() }) {
            Text("Back to Home")
        }
    }
  }
}
```

This button allows users to navigate back within the settings stack without affecting the other stacks.

Implementing Deep Links within Multi-Stack Navigation: When using multi-stack navigation, ensure that deep links can target specific stacks effectively. Define deep links in each NavHost as necessary.

Example:

```
composable(
    "settings/{settingId}",
    deepLinks = listOf(navDeepLink { uriPattern = "myapp://settings/{settingId}" })
) { backStackEntry ->
    val settingId = backStackEntry.arguments?.getString("settingId")
    SettingsDetailScreen(navController, settingId)
}
```

Here, deep links can be set to target specific screens within the settings stack, allowing users to jump directly into detailed settings.

Best Practices for Adaptive and Multi-Stack Navigation

Prioritize User Context: Design your navigation structure based on user context. Consider factors such as device type, screen size, and user behavior to create the most effective navigation experience.

Use Meaningful Navigation Destinations: Ensure that navigation destinations are logically organized and have meaningful names. This helps users understand where they are within the app.

Keep Navigation Simple: While multi-stack navigation can be powerful, ensure that your navigation remains intuitive. Avoid excessive complexity that could confuse users.

Test Across Devices: Regularly test your adaptive navigation on various device configurations to ensure that it works seamlessly and offers a consistent experience.

Maintain State Consistency: When using multiple navigation stacks, manage state carefully to avoid data loss or inconsistent UI across different parts of the app.

Handling adaptive and multi-stack navigation in Jetpack Compose enables developers to create flexible, user-friendly applications that cater to diverse user needs and device configurations. By implementing adaptive layouts and utilizing nested navigation hosts for multi-stack navigation, you can enhance user experience and improve the overall functionality of your app.

As you continue to develop your applications, keep in mind the principles and best practices discussed in this section to ensure that your navigation flows are intuitive, responsive, and efficient. Embracing these strategies will empower you to create a more engaging and streamlined experience for your users.

Chapter 4: Data Management with Room, LiveData, and ViewModel

In this chapter, we will delve into effective data management strategies for Android applications using Room, LiveData, and ViewModel—key components of the Android Jetpack architecture. You'll start by learning how to set up Room, Android's official persistence library, to create a robust local database for storing structured data. We will then explore how LiveData enables observable data changes, making it easy to update the UI in response to data changes without dealing with the complexities of lifecycle management. Additionally, you will discover the role of ViewModel in separating UI-related data from the Activity or Fragment lifecycle, ensuring data persistence across configuration changes. Through practical examples and best practices, this chapter will equip you with the knowledge to implement a clean and efficient data management layer in your apps, facilitating offline capabilities and improving overall user experience. By the end, you'll be ready to leverage these tools to build applications that handle data seamlessly and responsively.

4.1 Setting Up Room for Local Data Storage

Room is a powerful persistence library provided by Android, designed to facilitate local data storage in a structured and efficient manner. It serves as an abstraction layer over SQLite, making it easier for developers to work with databases while providing compile-time checks of SQLite queries. In this section, we will explore how to set up Room for local data storage, including defining entities, creating a database, and accessing data through data access objects (DAOs).

Understanding Room Architecture

Room consists of three primary components:

Entities: These represent the tables in your database. Each entity class corresponds to a table, and its fields correspond to the columns within that table.

Data Access Objects (DAOs): DAOs are Interfaces that define the methods for accessing the data in the database. They contain SQL queries that the Room library compiles and checks for correctness at compile time.

Database: The RoomDatabase class serves as the main access point to the underlying SQLite database. It contains the database holder and serves as the main point of interaction with the database.

Step-by-Step Guide to Setting Up Room

Step 1: Adding Room Dependencies

To use Room, you need to add the necessary dependencies to your build.gradle file. Include the following Room dependencies:

```
dependencies {
    def room_version = "2.5.0" // Check for the latest version

    implementation "androidx.room:room-runtime:$room_version"
    kapt "androidx.room:room-compiler:$room_version" // For Kotlin
    implementation "androidx.room:room-ktx:$room_version" // For Kotlin coroutines
support
}
```

Make sure you have the kapt plugin applied if you're using Kotlin:

```
apply plugin: 'kotlin-kapt'
```

Step 2: Defining Entities

Create entity classes to represent the tables in your database. Each entity class should be annotated with @Entity, and its fields should be annotated with @PrimaryKey or @ColumnInfo as needed.

Example:

```
import androidx.room.Entity
import androidx.room.PrimaryKey
import androidx.room.ColumnInfo

@Entity(tableName = "users")
data class User(
    @PrimaryKey(autoGenerate = true) val id: Long = 0,
    @ColumnInfo(name = "first_name") val firstName: String,
```

```
    @ColumnInfo(name = "last_name") val lastName: String,
    val age: Int
)
```

In this example, we create a User entity representing a table named users. The id field is the primary key, which will auto-generate.

Step 3: Creating Data Access Objects (DAOs)

Define DAOs to manage data access. DAOs should be interfaces or abstract classes annotated with @Dao. In this section, you will declare methods for performing database operations, such as insert, update, delete, and query.

Example:

```
import androidx.room.Dao
import androidx.room.Insert
import androidx.room.Update
import androidx.room.Delete
import androidx.room.Query

@Dao
interface UserDao {
    @Insert
    suspend fun insert(user: User)

    @Update
    suspend fun update(user: User)

    @Delete
    suspend fun delete(user: User)

    @Query("SELECT * FROM users WHERE id = :userId")
    suspend fun getUserById(userId: Long): User?

    @Query("SELECT * FROM users")
    suspend fun getAllUsers(): List<User>
}
```

In this example, the UserDao interface provides methods for inserting, updating, deleting, and querying User entities.

Step 4: Creating the Room Database

Next, create an abstract class that extends RoomDatabase and includes the database configuration. This class will serve as the main access point to your database.

Example:

```
import androidx.room.Database
import androidx.room.Room
import androidx.room.RoomDatabase
import android.content.Context

@Database(entities = [User::class], version = 1, exportSchema = false)
abstract class AppDatabase : RoomDatabase() {
    abstract fun userDao(): UserDao

    companion object {
        @Volatile
        private var INSTANCE: AppDatabase? = null

        fun getDatabase(context: Context): AppDatabase {
            return INSTANCE ?: synchronized(this) {
                val instance = Room.databaseBuilder(
                    context.applicationContext,
                    AppDatabase::class.java,
                    "app_database"
                ).build()
                INSTANCE = instance
                instance
            }
        }
    }
}
```

In this code snippet, we define the AppDatabase class, specifying the User entity and the database version. The getDatabase method provides a singleton instance of the database, ensuring that only one instance is created throughout the application's lifecycle.

Step 5: Accessing the Database

With the Room setup complete, you can now access the database through the DAO. Use coroutines or other asynchronous methods to perform database operations off the main thread.

Example:

```kotlin
import android.os.Bundle
import androidx.activity.ComponentActivity
import androidx.activity.compose.setContent
import androidx.lifecycle.lifecycleScope
import kotlinx.coroutines.launch

class MainActivity : ComponentActivity() {
    private val userDao: UserDao by lazy {
        AppDatabase.getDatabase(applicationContext).userDao()
    }

    override fun onCreate(savedInstanceState: Bundle?) {
        super.onCreate(savedInstanceState)
        setContent {
            // Your UI content goes here
        }

        // Example of inserting a user
        lifecycleScope.launch {
            val newUser = User(firstName = "John", lastName = "Doe", age = 30)
            userDao.insert(newUser)

            // Fetch all users
            val users = userDao.getAllUsers()
            // Use users in your UI
        }
    }
}
```

In this example, we use the lifecycleScope to launch a coroutine that inserts a new user and retrieves all users from the database.

Best Practices for Using Room

- **Use Coroutines**: Leverage Kotlin coroutines for asynchronous database operations to keep your UI responsive.
- **Keep Database Operations Off the Main Thread**: Ensure that all database queries and operations are performed off the main thread to avoid freezing the UI.
- **Versioning and Migrations**: When updating your database schema, always manage versioning and define migration strategies to prevent data loss.
- **Export Schema**: Set exportSchema to true in the @Database annotation to generate a schema file, which can help in maintaining database migrations.
- **Testing**: Write tests for your DAOs to ensure that database operations function as expected.

Setting up Room for local data storage in your Android application provides a robust and efficient way to manage data. By defining entities, creating DAOs, and establishing a database, you can easily implement persistent storage in your apps. The integration of Room with Jetpack Compose allows for a modern approach to building user interfaces that are responsive and data-driven. As you continue developing your application, remember to follow best practices to ensure a smooth and efficient data management experience.

4.2 Using LiveData and ViewModel for Observable Data

In Android development, managing UI-related data in a lifecycle-conscious way is crucial for creating responsive and robust applications. The combination of LiveData and ViewModel from the Android Architecture Components library provides a powerful framework for handling data in a way that respects the lifecycle of UI components. This section will explore how to effectively use LiveData and ViewModel to create observable data sources that enhance the user experience and simplify data management in Android applications.

Understanding LiveData

LiveData is a lifecycle-aware observable data holder class. It allows components (such as activities and fragments) to observe data changes and automatically update the UI when the data changes. One of the key benefits of LiveData is its ability to only notify active observers, which helps prevent memory leaks and crashes caused by updates to stopped or destroyed activities.

Key Characteristics of LiveData:

- **Lifecycle Awareness**: LiveData is aware of the lifecycle state of the UI components. It only updates active observers, avoiding unnecessary UI updates and resource wastage.
- **No Memory Leaks**: LiveData handles lifecycle management automatically, ensuring that it doesn't hold references to destroyed components, which helps prevent memory leaks.
- **Data Observability**: LiveData allows multiple observers to watch the same data, making it easy to update UI elements from various parts of your application.

Understanding ViewModel

ViewModel is designed to store and manage UI-related data in a lifecycle-conscious way. It survives configuration changes such as screen rotations, allowing data to be retained across UI component lifecycles. ViewModel instances are scoped to the lifecycle of the associated UI component, which helps manage complex UI data and operations.

Key Characteristics of ViewModel:

- **Lifecycle Awareness**: ViewModel is designed to outlive the lifecycle of UI components, making it ideal for managing data that needs to persist across configuration changes.
- **Separation of Concerns**: By separating the UI logic from the data management logic, ViewModels promote a cleaner architecture, making the code more maintainable and testable.
- **No Context Reference**: ViewModels should not hold references to Views or Activities, helping to prevent memory leaks.

Setting Up LiveData and ViewModel

Step 1: Add Dependencies

To use LiveData and ViewModel, ensure you have the necessary dependencies in your build.gradle file:

```
dependencies {
    def lifecycle_version = "2.5.0" // Check for the latest version
    implementation "androidx.lifecycle:lifecycle-viewmodel-ktx:$lifecycle_version"
```

```
    implementation "androidx.lifecycle:lifecycle-livedata-ktx:$lifecycle_version"
}
```

Step 2: Create a ViewModel

Define a ViewModel class that will hold your data. The ViewModel will expose LiveData objects that the UI can observe.

Example:

```
import androidx.lifecycle.LiveData
import androidx.lifecycle.MutableLiveData
import androidx.lifecycle.ViewModel

class UserViewModel : ViewModel() {
    // Private mutable LiveData
    private val _user = MutableLiveData<User>()

    // Public LiveData
    val user: LiveData<User> get() = _user

    // Method to update user data
    fun updateUser(newUser: User) {
        _user.value = newUser
    }
}
```

In this example, UserViewModel holds a private MutableLiveData instance for the User data and exposes it as LiveData. This encapsulation prevents direct modification from outside the ViewModel.

Step 3: Observing LiveData in UI Components

To observe LiveData changes in your UI components, you typically do this within an Activity or Fragment. When the observed data changes, the UI will automatically update.

Example:

```
import androidx.activity.ComponentActivity
import androidx.activity.compose.setContent
```

```kotlin
import androidx.activity.viewModels
import androidx.compose.material.Text
import androidx.compose.runtime.Composable
import androidx.compose.runtime.LaunchedEffect
import androidx.compose.runtime.collectAsState
import androidx.lifecycle.Observer

class MainActivity : ComponentActivity() {
    private val userViewModel: UserViewModel by viewModels()

    override fun onCreate(savedInstanceState: Bundle?) {
        super.onCreate(savedInstanceState)
        setContent {
            // Observing user LiveData
            val user = userViewModel.user.observeAsState()

            // Displaying user information
            user.value?.let {
                UserScreen(it)
            }
        }
    }
}

@Composable
fun UserScreen(user: User) {
    Text(text = "User Name: ${user.firstName} ${user.lastName}")
}
```

In this example, we create an Activity that observes the user LiveData from UserViewModel. The UI is updated automatically whenever the user data changes.

Step 4: Updating LiveData

To update the LiveData, you can call methods in your ViewModel, which will automatically notify the observers.

Example:

```
// Update user information
```

```
userViewModel.updateUser(User(firstName = "Jane", lastName = "Doe", age = 25))
```

When you call updateUser(), any UI component observing the user LiveData will receive the update and refresh accordingly.

Best Practices for Using LiveData and ViewModel

Encapsulate Mutable LiveData: Always expose LiveData as immutable to prevent unwanted changes from outside the ViewModel.

Use ViewModel for Data Logic: Keep data handling logic within ViewModels. This maintains a clear separation between UI and data layers.

Handle Configuration Changes: Leverage ViewModel's lifecycle-aware nature to retain data during configuration changes without manual data restoration.

Avoid Long Operations on LiveData: If you need to perform long operations or background tasks, consider using Coroutines or other threading techniques, and update LiveData once the operation completes.

Testing: Write unit tests for your ViewModels to verify data management and LiveData behavior, ensuring reliability in your application.

Using LiveData and ViewModel in Android development enhances the way you manage and observe data in your applications. LiveData's lifecycle-awareness and ViewModel's ability to survive configuration changes make them an ideal pair for handling UI-related data efficiently. By following best practices and leveraging these components effectively, you can create responsive and robust Android applications that provide a seamless user experience. As you continue to develop your applications, integrating LiveData and ViewModel will simplify data management and improve your app's architecture.

4.3 Advanced Data Flows: Repository Pattern and Offline Sync

In modern Android applications, effective data management is crucial for creating responsive and user-friendly interfaces. The Repository Pattern combined with offline synchronization techniques provides a robust architecture for managing data from multiple sources, ensuring a seamless user experience even in scenarios of limited connectivity. This section will explore the Repository Pattern and how to implement offline sync strategies in your Android applications.

Understanding the Repository Pattern

The Repository Pattern serves as an abstraction layer between the data sources and the rest of the application. It centralizes data management, making it easier to handle data from various sources such as local databases, network APIs, or caches. By isolating data access logic, the Repository Pattern promotes a cleaner architecture and simplifies unit testing.

Key Characteristics of the Repository Pattern:

- **Single Responsibility**: Each repository focuses solely on data management, separating concerns and making the codebase more maintainable.
- **Data Abstraction**: The repository abstracts the underlying data sources (local or remote), allowing the rest of the application to interact with a consistent API regardless of where the data is coming from.
- **Improved Testability**: By mocking repositories during unit tests, you can easily simulate various data scenarios without relying on actual data sources.

Implementing the Repository Pattern

Step 1: Define Data Models

Start by defining your data models that represent the structure of the data you will be working with. For example, consider a simple User model:

```
data class User(
    val id: Long,
    val firstName: String,
    val lastName: String,
    val age: Int
)
```

Step 2: Create Data Sources

Define your data sources, which could include local databases (e.g., Room) and remote APIs (e.g., Retrofit). For this example, we'll create a local data source and a remote data source.

Local Data Source (Room):

```kotlin
interface UserLocalDataSource {
    suspend fun getUserById(id: Long): User?
    suspend fun saveUser(user: User)
}

class UserLocalDataSourceImpl(private val userDao: UserDao) : UserLocalDataSource
{
    override suspend fun getUserById(id: Long): User? = userDao.getUserById(id)
    override suspend fun saveUser(user: User) = userDao.insert(user)
}
```

Remote Data Source (Retrofit):

```kotlin
interface UserRemoteDataSource {
    suspend fun fetchUser(id: Long): User
}

class UserRemoteDataSourceImpl(private val userApi: UserApi) :
UserRemoteDataSource {
    override suspend fun fetchUser(id: Long): User = userApi.getUser(id)
}
```

Step 3: Create the Repository

Next, implement the repository that combines the local and remote data sources. The repository will manage data flow and perform caching or synchronization logic as needed.

```kotlin
class UserRepository(
    private val localDataSource: UserLocalDataSource,
    private val remoteDataSource: UserRemoteDataSource
) {
    suspend fun getUser(id: Long): User? {
        // Attempt to get user from local data source first
        val localUser = localDataSource.getUserById(id)
        return localUser ?: fetchUserFromRemote(id)
    }
```

```
private suspend fun fetchUserFromRemote(id: Long): User {
    val remoteUser = remoteDataSource.fetchUser(id)
    localDataSource.saveUser(remoteUser) // Cache the result locally
    return remoteUser
  }
}
```

In this example, the UserRepository first attempts to retrieve the user from the local data source. If the user is not found, it fetches the data from the remote source and caches it locally.

Step 4: Integrating the Repository with ViewModel

Incorporate the repository into your ViewModel, allowing your UI to observe changes and respond accordingly.

```
class UserViewModel(private val userRepository: UserRepository) : ViewModel() {
    private val _user = MutableLiveData<User>()
    val user: LiveData<User> get() = _user

    fun loadUser(id: Long) {
        viewModelScope.launch {
            _user.value = userRepository.getUser(id)
        }
    }
}
```

Implementing Offline Sync

Offline sync strategies ensure that your application remains functional even without an internet connection. This involves managing local data storage, syncing changes when the network is available, and providing users with feedback during synchronization processes.

Step 1: Local Cache Management

To manage local data caching, ensure that your repository retrieves data from the local database when offline. If a user makes changes while offline, store those changes locally and synchronize them later.

```
suspend fun updateUser(user: User) {
    localDataSource.saveUser(user)
    // Sync with remote if online
    if (isNetworkAvailable()) {
        syncUserWithRemote(user)
    }
}

private suspend fun syncUserWithRemote(user: User) {
    try {
        remoteDataSource.updateUser(user)
    } catch (e: Exception) {
        // Handle sync failure (optional: notify the user)
    }
}
```

Step 2: Handling Network Connectivity

Use a ConnectivityManager or a third-party library (like WorkManager) to listen for network changes. This allows you to trigger sync operations whenever the device reconnects to the internet.

```
fun registerNetworkCallback() {
    val connectivityManager = getSystemService(Context.CONNECTIVITY_SERVICE)
as ConnectivityManager
    val builder = NetworkRequest.Builder()

    connectivityManager.registerNetworkCallback(builder.build(), object :
ConnectivityManager.NetworkCallback() {
        override fun onAvailable(network: Network) {
            super.onAvailable(network)
            // Trigger sync operations here
            viewModel.syncDataWithRemote()
        }
    })
}
```

Step 3: Providing User Feedback

User experience is essential, especially during synchronization. Implement a progress indicator or a notification system to inform users about the sync status.

```
private fun showSyncProgress() {
    // Update UI to show progress (e.g., a loading spinner)
}

private fun showSyncComplete() {
    // Update UI to indicate sync is complete
}
```

Best Practices for Using the Repository Pattern and Offline Sync

Use Coroutine for Asynchronous Operations: Employ Kotlin Coroutines for non-blocking database and network operations to keep your UI responsive.

Separate Concerns: Maintain a clear separation of concerns by defining data sources, repositories, and ViewModels distinctly.

Handle Errors Gracefully: Implement robust error handling and provide feedback to users in case of failures during data operations or network sync.

Use WorkManager for Sync Tasks: Leverage WorkManager for scheduling background tasks that require reliable execution, especially for sync operations.

Optimize Network Calls: Implement caching strategies and conditional requests to minimize unnecessary data transfers and improve performance.

The Repository Pattern combined with offline synchronization techniques is essential for building modern Android applications that manage data efficiently. By isolating data access logic within repositories and implementing strategies for offline data management, you can create applications that remain functional and responsive, even in challenging network conditions. As you develop your Android applications, employing these patterns will help you maintain clean architecture, enhance testability, and provide a superior user experience. Integrating these practices into your projects will empower you to build robust, resilient applications that keep users engaged and satisfied, regardless of connectivity.

Chapter 5: Networking and API Integration with Retrofit and RESTful APIs

In this chapter, we will focus on the essential aspects of networking and API integration in Android applications, using Retrofit, a powerful type-safe HTTP client. You will learn how to set up Retrofit to simplify the process of making network requests and parsing JSON responses from RESTful APIs. We'll explore how to configure different HTTP methods, manage query parameters, and handle authentication seamlessly. Additionally, we will discuss error handling strategies and the importance of implementing robust caching mechanisms to enhance performance and user experience. As we delve into real-world examples, you'll gain insights into optimizing network calls and working with asynchronous responses, ensuring your applications remain responsive even when fetching data from remote sources. By the end of this chapter, you will have the skills to effectively integrate and manage network operations, allowing you to build feature-rich applications that interact smoothly with external services.

5.1 Configuring Retrofit for API Calls and Customizing Requests

In the landscape of Android development, Retrofit stands out as a powerful library for making network requests and handling API calls efficiently. Its flexibility and ease of use make it a go-to choice for developers aiming to interact with RESTful APIs. This section will guide you through configuring Retrofit for API calls, customizing requests, and managing responses effectively.

Understanding Retrofit

Retrofit is a type-safe HTTP client for Android and Java, developed by Square. It simplifies the process of making network requests by converting HTTP API into a Java interface. Retrofit supports various request types (GET, POST, PUT, DELETE), enables automatic conversion of responses, and facilitates the integration of custom headers, query parameters, and more.

Step 1: Adding Dependencies

To start using Retrofit in your Android project, you need to include the necessary dependencies in your build.gradle file:

```
dependencies {
    implementation 'com.squareup.retrofit2:retrofit:2.9.0' // Check for the latest version
    implementation 'com.squareup.retrofit2:converter-gson:2.9.0' // For JSON conversion
    implementation 'com.squareup.okhttp3:logging-interceptor:4.9.1' // Optional logging
}
```

The converter-gson dependency allows Retrofit to automatically serialize and deserialize JSON data, making it easy to work with REST APIs.

Step 2: Creating a Retrofit Instance

Before making API calls, you need to create a Retrofit instance. This involves specifying the base URL of the API and configuring a converter factory.

```
import retrofit2.Retrofit
import retrofit2.converter.gson.GsonConverterFactory

object RetrofitClient {
    private const val BASE_URL = "https://api.example.com/"

    val retrofit: Retrofit = Retrofit.Builder()
        .baseUrl(BASE_URL)
        .addConverterFactory(GsonConverterFactory.create()) // Convert JSON to Kotlin
objects
        .build()
}
```

In this code snippet, we create a singleton instance of Retrofit with the specified base URL and a Gson converter.

Step 3: Defining API Endpoints

Next, define an interface that outlines the API endpoints you want to access. Each method in the interface represents a specific HTTP request.

Example API Interface:

```
import retrofit2.http.GET
import retrofit2.http.Path
```

```kotlin
import retrofit2.http.Query
import retrofit2.Call

interface ApiService {

    // Fetch user details by ID
    @GET("users/{id}")
    fun getUserById(@Path("id") userId: Long): Call<User>

    // Fetch a list of users with optional query parameters
    @GET("users")
    fun getUsers(@Query("page") page: Int, @Query("size") size: Int): Call<List<User>>

    // Create a new user
    @POST("users")
    fun createUser(@Body user: User): Call<User>
}
```

In this interface, we define three endpoints: one to get a user by ID, another to fetch a list of users with pagination, and a third to create a new user. Each method specifies the HTTP method, the endpoint, and any parameters.

Step 4: Making API Calls

To make an API call, you need to create an instance of your API service and invoke the appropriate method. Retrofit will handle the network request asynchronously.

Example of Making a Call:

```kotlin
import retrofit2.Call
import retrofit2.Callback
import retrofit2.Response

val apiService = RetrofitClient.retrofit.create(ApiService::class.java)

// Fetch user by ID
apiService.getUserById(1).enqueue(object : Callback<User> {
    override fun onResponse(call: Call<User>, response: Response<User>) {
        if (response.isSuccessful) {
            val user = response.body()
```

```
        // Handle the user data
    } else {
        // Handle error response
    }
}

override fun onFailure(call: Call<User>, t: Throwable) {
    // Handle failure
}
})
```

In this example, we fetch a user by ID using the getUserById method and enqueue the call. Retrofit handles threading for us, executing the request in the background and returning the result in a callback.

Step 5: Customizing Requests

Retrofit provides various ways to customize your API requests, such as adding headers, query parameters, and timeouts.

1. Adding Headers

You can add common headers to every request by using an Interceptor or directly in the API method.

Using an Interceptor:

```
import okhttp3.OkHttpClient

val client = OkHttpClient.Builder()
    .addInterceptor { chain ->
        val original = chain.request()
        val request = original.newBuilder()
            .header("Authorization", "Bearer your_token")
            .method(original.method(), original.body())
            .build()
        chain.proceed(request)
    }
    .build()
```

```
val retrofit = Retrofit.Builder()
    .baseUrl(BASE_URL)
    .client(client) // Set the custom client
    .addConverterFactory(GsonConverterFactory.create())
    .build()
```

In this example, we add an Authorization header to every request by intercepting the request chain.

2. Customizing Timeout Settings

You can customize the timeout settings for your requests as well:

```
val client = OkHttpClient.Builder()
    .connectTimeout(30, TimeUnit.SECONDS)
    .readTimeout(30, TimeUnit.SECONDS)
    .writeTimeout(30, TimeUnit.SECONDS)
    .build()
```

By setting these timeout values, you can ensure that your application handles slow network conditions gracefully.

3. Handling Responses

Retrofit supports various response types, allowing you to handle JSON, XML, or other formats. To handle the response in a type-safe manner, you can define response classes that map to the expected JSON structure.

Example Response Class:

```
data class User(
    val id: Long,
    val firstName: String,
    val lastName: String,
    val age: Int
)
```

By using data classes, you enable Retrofit to automatically map JSON responses to Kotlin objects, simplifying your code.

Best Practices for Using Retrofit

Use Coroutines: Consider using Kotlin Coroutines with Retrofit to manage asynchronous calls more elegantly and reduce callback hell. You can replace Call<T> with suspend fun in your API interface.

Error Handling: Implement comprehensive error handling for your API calls, including parsing error responses and managing network failures.

Caching Responses: Use caching mechanisms to improve performance and reduce unnecessary network calls, especially for frequently accessed data.

Modular API Services: Split your API services into separate interfaces based on functionality or feature areas to keep your code organized.

Unit Testing: Write unit tests for your API service to ensure the correctness of your request and response handling.

Configuring Retrofit for API calls and customizing requests is a crucial skill for any Android developer. By leveraging Retrofit's capabilities, you can streamline the process of making network requests and efficiently manage API interactions. The flexibility offered by Retrofit allows you to handle different data formats, add custom headers, and manage responses easily. As you integrate Retrofit into your applications, follow best practices to ensure a robust and maintainable codebase, ultimately enhancing your application's performance and user experience. With a strong understanding of Retrofit, you'll be well-equipped to tackle complex networking tasks in your Android projects.

5.2 Handling API Responses and Error Management

When building Android applications that interact with RESTful APIs, handling API responses and managing errors effectively is essential for delivering a seamless user experience. This section focuses on how to handle different types of API responses, implement robust error management strategies, and ensure that your application can gracefully handle failures and unexpected situations.

Understanding API Responses

API responses can vary significantly based on the endpoint being called and the data being retrieved. Typically, responses include:

- **Success Responses**: Indicate that the request was successful, often returning the requested data.
- **Error Responses**: Indicate that something went wrong, providing information about the nature of the error.
- **Empty Responses**: Situations where a request is successful, but there is no data to return.

When interacting with APIs, it's vital to correctly interpret these responses to provide appropriate feedback to the user.

Handling Successful Responses

When a successful response is received, you generally want to extract the data and update the UI accordingly. Here's how to do that with Retrofit.

1. Using Callbacks

Using Retrofit's enqueue method, you can handle API responses asynchronously. Here's an example of how to handle a successful response:

```
apiService.getUserById(1).enqueue(object : Callback<User> {
    override fun onResponse(call: Call<User>, response: Response<User>) {
        if (response.isSuccessful) {
            val user = response.body()
            user?.let {
                // Update the UI with user data
                updateUI(it)
            } ?: run {
                // Handle the case where the response is successful but the body is null
                showEmptyDataMessage()
            }
        } else {
            // Handle HTTP error responses
            handleHttpError(response.code())
        }
    }

    override fun onFailure(call: Call<User>, t: Throwable) {
        // Handle network failure
```

```
        handleNetworkError(t)
    }
})
```

In this example, we check if the response is successful using response.isSuccessful. If it is, we retrieve the user data. If the body is null, we handle it accordingly. For unsuccessful responses, we pass the HTTP status code to an error handler.

2. Using Coroutines

For a more modern approach, you can use Kotlin Coroutines to handle responses more cleanly:

```
viewModelScope.launch {
    try {
        val user = apiService.getUserById(1).awaitResponse()
        // Update the UI with user data
        updateUI(user.body()!!)
    } catch (e: Exception) {
        // Handle network failure
        handleNetworkError(e)
    }
}
```

Here, awaitResponse() allows you to retrieve the response as a suspend function, simplifying asynchronous code flow.

Handling Error Responses

Error handling is crucial to maintaining a good user experience. Here are the common error scenarios and how to handle them:

1. HTTP Errors

When a request fails due to a client or server error (status codes 4xx or 5xx), it's essential to provide feedback to the user. Here's how to handle HTTP errors based on the response code:

```
fun handleHttpError(code: Int) {
    when (code) {
```

```
    400 -> showErrorMessage("Bad Request: Please check your input.")
    401 -> showErrorMessage("Unauthorized: Please log in.")
    404 -> showErrorMessage("Not Found: The requested resource could not be
found.")
    500 -> showErrorMessage("Server Error: Please try again later.")
    else -> showErrorMessage("Unexpected Error: Please try again.")
  }
}
```

In this function, we provide specific feedback based on the HTTP status code returned from the server, helping users understand what went wrong.

2. Network Failures

Network-related issues can occur for various reasons, such as no internet connection or timeouts. Use the onFailure callback to handle these cases:

```
override fun onFailure(call: Call<User>, t: Throwable) {
    handleNetworkError(t)
}

fun handleNetworkError(t: Throwable) {
    if (t is IOException) {
        showErrorMessage("Network error: Please check your connection.")
    } else {
        showErrorMessage("Unexpected error: ${t.localizedMessage}")
    }
}
```

Here, we differentiate between IO exceptions (indicative of network issues) and other unexpected exceptions, providing tailored feedback to the user.

Managing Empty Responses

In some cases, an API call may succeed but return no data. It's essential to handle this scenario gracefully.

```
if (response.isSuccessful) {
    val users = response.body()
    if (users.isNullOrEmpty()) {
```

```
        showEmptyDataMessage()
    } else {
        updateUI(users)
    }
}
```

In this example, we check if the response body is null or empty and inform the user if there are no results to display.

Logging and Monitoring Errors

Monitoring errors is vital for debugging and improving the user experience. Use logging libraries to record API calls and errors for later analysis. For example, you can use Timber for logging:

Timber.e("Error fetching user: ${t.localizedMessage}")

Integrating error logging will help you track issues in production and improve your application over time.

Best Practices for API Response Handling and Error Management

Consistent Error Messages: Ensure that error messages are consistent and user-friendly. Avoid technical jargon; use language that your users can understand.

Use a Global Error Handler: Consider implementing a global error handler to catch and manage errors in one place, making it easier to maintain and update error handling logic.

Retry Mechanism: Implement a retry mechanism for transient errors (e.g., network timeouts) to improve user experience without requiring manual intervention.

Timeouts and Caching: Set appropriate timeouts for your network requests and consider caching strategies to improve performance and reduce reliance on the network.

Unit Testing: Write unit tests for your API response handling logic to ensure that various scenarios are covered, including successful responses, HTTP errors, and network failures.

Handling API responses and managing errors effectively is crucial for any Android application that interacts with remote services. By understanding how to deal with successful responses, HTTP errors, network failures, and empty responses, you can create a robust and user-friendly application. Implementing best practices for error management will not only enhance the user experience but also help you maintain a cleaner, more maintainable codebase. With proper handling of API responses and errors, your application will be well-equipped to provide a smooth and reliable user experience, even in the face of network challenges and unexpected situations.

5.3 Optimizing Network Performance with Caching and WebSockets

Optimizing network performance is crucial for building responsive and efficient Android applications that interact with RESTful APIs. Two powerful strategies to enhance performance are caching and utilizing WebSockets. This section will explore how to effectively implement caching mechanisms to reduce network calls and enhance user experience, as well as how to leverage WebSockets for real-time communication in your applications.

Understanding Caching in Android

Caching is a technique used to store frequently accessed data locally, which minimizes the need for repeated network requests. By caching data, applications can improve load times, reduce latency, and save bandwidth. Android provides various mechanisms for caching data fetched from APIs, with Retrofit and OkHttp being prominent tools.

Types of Caching

- **Memory Caching**: Temporarily stores data in RAM for quick access during an app's runtime. While this is fast, it is volatile and will be lost when the app is killed.
- **Disk Caching**: Stores data on the device's storage. This is slower than memory caching but persists even when the app is closed, making it ideal for offline access.

Implementing Caching with Retrofit and OkHttp

To implement caching using Retrofit and OkHttp, follow these steps:

Step 1: Configure OkHttp Client for Caching

Add caching capabilities to your OkHttp client by defining a cache directory and setting the maximum cache size.

```
import okhttp3.Cache
import okhttp3.OkHttpClient

val cacheSize = 10 * 1024 * 1024 // 10 MiB
val cacheDir = File(context.cacheDir, "httpCache")
val cache = Cache(cacheDir, cacheSize)

val client = OkHttpClient.Builder()
  .cache(cache) // Set the cache
  .build()

val retrofit = Retrofit.Builder()
  .baseUrl(BASE_URL)
  .client(client) // Use the custom client with cache
  .addConverterFactory(GsonConverterFactory.create())
  .build()
```

Step 2: Control Cache Behavior with HTTP Headers

To make effective use of the cache, control caching behavior using HTTP headers:

- **Cache-Control**: Directives that control how, and for how long, responses can be cached.
- **Expires**: A timestamp indicating when the cached response is considered stale.

```
@GET("users")
suspend fun getUsers(@Query("page") page: Int): Response<List<User>>
```

Make sure your server responds with appropriate caching headers. For example, you can configure your server to include headers like:

```
Cache-Control: public, max-age=3600
```

This tells the client to cache the response for 3600 seconds (1 hour).

Benefits of Caching

- **Reduced Network Latency**: By serving cached data, your application can quickly display information without waiting for network responses.
- **Improved User Experience**: Users can access data even when offline or with poor network connections.
- **Reduced Bandwidth Usage**: Caching helps decrease the amount of data sent over the network, leading to cost savings and better performance.

Using WebSockets for Real-Time Communication

While caching is beneficial for reducing API calls, there are scenarios where real-time data updates are essential, such as chat applications, notifications, and live data feeds. WebSockets provide a full-duplex communication channel over a single, long-lived connection, enabling real-time data transfer between clients and servers.

Benefits of WebSockets

- **Reduced Latency**: WebSockets maintain an open connection, allowing immediate data transfer without the overhead of establishing new connections for each request.
- **Efficiency**: Unlike traditional HTTP requests, which involve headers and separate connections for each interaction, WebSockets allow data to be sent back and forth in a more efficient manner.
- **Real-Time Updates**: WebSockets are ideal for applications that require instant updates, such as live sports scores, chat applications, and stock tickers.

Implementing WebSockets in Android

To use WebSockets in your Android application, you can utilize libraries such as OkHttp (which supports WebSockets out of the box) or Socket.IO for added features.

Using OkHttp for WebSockets:

Add Dependency: Ensure you have the OkHttp dependency in your build.gradle file:

implementation 'com.squareup.okhttp3:okhttp:4.9.1'

Establishing a WebSocket Connection:

Here's how to create a WebSocket connection using OkHttp:

```kotlin
val client = OkHttpClient()

val request = Request.Builder()
    .url("wss://your.websocket.url")
    .build()

val webSocket = client.newWebSocket(request, object : WebSocketListener() {
    override fun onOpen(webSocket: WebSocket, response: Response) {
        // Handle connection opened
    }

    override fun onMessage(webSocket: WebSocket, text: String) {
        // Handle incoming message
    }

    override fun onFailure(webSocket: WebSocket, t: Throwable, response: Response?)
{
        // Handle connection failure
    }
})

// Don't forget to close the connection when done
webSocket.close(1000, "Closing connection")
```

Sending Messages:

You can send messages through the WebSocket connection as follows:

```kotlin
webSocket.send("Hello, WebSocket!")
```

Best Practices for Using Caching and WebSockets

Combine Caching with WebSockets: Use caching for static or infrequently updated data and WebSockets for dynamic or real-time data. For example, cache user profiles while using WebSockets for live chat messages.

Implement Expiration Logic: For cached data, implement logic to check data freshness and decide when to refresh the cache by fetching new data from the server.

Graceful Fallbacks: In case of WebSocket disconnections, implement a fallback mechanism to revert to REST API calls if real-time updates are lost temporarily.

Error Handling: Ensure you have robust error handling for both caching failures and WebSocket connections to maintain a good user experience.

Performance Monitoring: Regularly monitor network performance and optimize cache size and WebSocket message handling to keep your application responsive.

Optimizing network performance in Android applications is essential for creating responsive and user-friendly experiences. By implementing caching strategies, you can significantly reduce the number of network calls, improve load times, and save bandwidth. Additionally, leveraging WebSockets allows your application to maintain real-time communication with servers, providing instant updates and enhancing user engagement. Together, these techniques form a robust foundation for handling networking in Android applications, enabling developers to build high-performing and responsive apps. As you implement these strategies, always consider best practices to ensure a seamless and efficient user experience.

Chapter 6: Dependency Injection with Dagger and Hilt

In this chapter, we will explore the principles and practices of dependency injection (DI) in Android development, focusing on Dagger and its newer counterpart, Hilt. You will learn why dependency injection is essential for building scalable and testable applications, helping to reduce tight coupling between components. We'll start with the fundamentals of Dagger, discussing how to configure modules and components to provide dependencies throughout your application. Then, we'll transition to Hilt, which simplifies the DI process by offering a more streamlined approach with built-in support for Android components. You will see how Hilt manages the lifecycle of dependencies and provides convenient annotations to minimize boilerplate code. Through practical examples, we'll cover advanced topics such as multibinding, qualifiers, and scope management, equipping you with the tools needed to implement effective dependency injection strategies in your projects. By the end of this chapter, you will have a solid understanding of how to leverage Dagger and Hilt to create modular, maintainable, and easily testable Android applications.

6.1 Understanding Dependency Injection and Scoping

Dependency Injection (DI) is a design pattern that enables developers to manage and control the dependencies between components in an application. By using DI, you can create more modular, testable, and maintainable code. In the context of Android development, DI has become an essential practice, particularly with the rise of frameworks like Dagger and Hilt, which automate much of the boilerplate associated with managing dependencies. This section will cover the fundamental concepts of dependency injection, the different types of DI, and the importance of scoping in the DI process.

What is Dependency Injection?

At its core, dependency injection is a technique in which an object (or class) receives its dependencies from an external source rather than creating them internally. This approach promotes loose coupling and separation of concerns, which are vital for creating scalable and maintainable applications.

Example of Dependency Injection:

Consider a simple scenario where you have a UserRepository that depends on a UserService to fetch user data. Without dependency injection, the UserRepository might instantiate UserService directly:

```kotlin
class UserRepository {
    private val userService = UserService() // Tight coupling

    fun getUser(id: String): User {
        return userService.fetchUser(id)
    }
}
```
In contrast, with dependency injection, you can pass the UserService as a parameter, allowing for greater flexibility and testability:

```kotlin
kotlin
Copy code
class UserRepository(private val userService: UserService) {
    fun getUser(id: String): User {
        return userService.fetchUser(id)
    }
}
```

In this revised version, UserRepository does not need to know how to create a UserService, which makes it easier to substitute different implementations (such as a mock service for testing).

Types of Dependency Injection

Constructor Injection: This is the most common method of dependency injection. Dependencies are provided through the class constructor. It promotes immutability and ensures that a class is always initialized with its dependencies.

```kotlin
class UserRepository @Inject constructor(private val userService: UserService) {
    // ...
}
```

Setter Injection: In this approach, dependencies are provided through setter methods. This method is useful for optional dependencies that may not always be required.

```
class UserRepository {
    private lateinit var userService: UserService

    @Inject
    fun setUserService(userService: UserService) {
        this.userService = userService
    }
}
```

Interface Injection: This is less common and involves defining an interface for injecting dependencies. This method can add unnecessary complexity and is not widely adopted in modern Android development.

Benefits of Dependency Injection

- **Decoupling**: By removing direct dependencies, classes can evolve independently of each other, making the code easier to maintain.
- **Testability**: DI simplifies unit testing since you can easily substitute mock objects for dependencies, allowing for isolated tests.
- **Configuration Flexibility**: DI enables you to change the implementation of a dependency without altering the code that uses it. This is particularly useful for switching between production and test implementations.

Understanding Scoping

In dependency injection, scoping refers to the lifecycle of the dependencies being injected. It defines how long an instance of a dependency should live and when it should be created or destroyed. Properly managing the scope of dependencies is crucial for resource management, performance, and avoiding memory leaks.

Common Scopes in Dependency Injection

Singleton Scope: A singleton-scoped dependency is created once and shared across the entire application. It is ideal for stateless components or services that should have a single instance throughout the app's lifecycle.

```
@Singleton
class UserService @Inject constructor() {
    // Implementation details
}
```

Activity Scope: Dependencies marked with activity scope are created when an activity is created and destroyed when the activity is finished. This is useful for dependencies that should only exist during the lifetime of a single activity.

```
@ActivityScoped
class UserViewModel @Inject constructor(private val userRepository: UserRepository) {
    // Implementation details
}
```

Fragment Scope: Similar to activity scope, but dependencies exist only during the lifecycle of a fragment. This scope is useful for managing dependencies that should only be available within a fragment.

```
@FragmentScoped
class UserFragment : Fragment() {
    @Inject
    lateinit var userViewModel: UserViewModel
}
```

ViewModel Scope: In Android, view models are often used to hold UI-related data. Dependencies defined with view model scope will live as long as the view model does, making it suitable for UI logic and data that should survive configuration changes.

```
@ViewModelScoped
class UserViewModel @Inject constructor(private val userRepository: UserRepository) :
ViewModel() {
    // Implementation details
}
```

Implementing Dependency Injection with Dagger and Hilt

Dagger

Dagger is a popular dependency injection framework for Java and Android. It requires you to define components and modules explicitly. Here's a simple Dagger setup:

Define a Module: A module provides the dependencies.

```
@Module
```

```kotlin
class UserModule {
    @Provides
    @Singleton
    fun provideUserService(): UserService {
        return UserService()
    }
}
```

Define a Component: A component connects the module to the classes that require dependencies.

```kotlin
@Singleton
@Component(modules = [UserModule::class])
interface AppComponent {
    fun inject(application: MyApplication)
}
```

Inject Dependencies: Use the component to inject dependencies where needed.

```kotlin
class MyApplication : Application() {
    @Inject
    lateinit var userService: UserService

    override fun onCreate() {
        super.onCreate()
        DaggerAppComponent.create().inject(this)
    }
}
```

Hilt

Hilt is built on top of Dagger and simplifies DI setup in Android applications by providing annotations and reducing boilerplate code.

Add Hilt Dependencies: Ensure you have Hilt dependencies in your build.gradle file.

```
implementation "com.google.dagger:hilt-android:2.x"
kapt "com.google.dagger:hilt-compiler:2.x"
```

Enable Hilt in the Application Class:

```kotlin
@HiltAndroidApp
class MyApplication : Application()
```
Inject Dependencies Using Hilt:

```kotlin
kotlin
Copy code
@AndroidEntryPoint
class MainActivity : AppCompatActivity() {
    @Inject
    lateinit var userService: UserService

    override fun onCreate(savedInstanceState: Bundle?) {
        super.onCreate(savedInstanceState)
        setContentView(R.layout.activity_main)
    }
}
```

Best Practices for Dependency Injection

- **Limit Scope**: Use the most appropriate scope for your dependencies to manage memory efficiently and avoid leaks.
- **Favor Constructor Injection**: Prefer constructor injection for mandatory dependencies to enforce immutability and simplify testing.
- **Keep Modules Focused**: Each module should focus on a specific functionality or domain to enhance readability and maintainability.
- **Use Qualifiers for Multiple Implementations**: If you have multiple implementations of a dependency, use qualifiers to differentiate them clearly.

Understanding dependency injection and scoping is fundamental to building robust and maintainable Android applications. By decoupling components and managing their lifecycles effectively, developers can create modular, testable code that is easier to maintain and extend over time. Utilizing frameworks like Dagger and Hilt simplifies the implementation of dependency injection, enabling developers to focus on building features rather than managing dependencies. As you integrate DI into your Android projects, following best practices will help ensure your code remains clean, efficient, and scalable.

6.2 Setting Up Dagger and Hilt in an Android Project

Dependency Injection (DI) is a powerful design pattern that can significantly enhance the modularity, testability, and maintainability of your Android applications. Dagger and Hilt are two popular frameworks used for implementing DI in Android. Dagger is a fully featured DI framework, while Hilt, built on top of Dagger, simplifies the process of dependency injection specifically for Android apps. In this section, we will walk through the steps required to set up Dagger and Hilt in an Android project, including configurations, annotations, and basic usage.

Step 1: Adding Dependencies

To get started with Hilt in your Android project, you need to add the required dependencies in your build.gradle files.

Project-level build.gradle: Make sure you have the Google Maven repository included.

```
buildscript {
  repositories {
    google() // Required for Hilt
    mavenCentral()
  }
  dependencies {
    classpath "com.android.tools.build:gradle:7.x.x"
    classpath "com.google.dagger:hilt-android-gradle-plugin:2.x" // Hilt plugin
  }
}
```

Module-level build.gradle: Add Hilt dependencies and the KAPT plugin to the android module.

```
apply plugin: 'kotlin-kapt' // Ensure Kotlin KAPT is applied
```

```
dependencies {
  implementation "com.google.dagger:hilt-android:2.x" // Hilt library
  kapt "com.google.dagger:hilt-compiler:2.x" // Hilt compiler

  // Optionally, include Dagger dependencies if using Dagger alongside Hilt
  implementation "com.google.dagger:dagger:2.x"
  kapt "com.google.dagger:dagger-compiler:2.x"
```

```
}
```

Replace 2.x with the latest stable version of Hilt and Dagger available in the official documentation.

Step 2: Enabling Hilt in Your Application

To start using Hilt, you need to annotate your application class with @HiltAndroidApp. This annotation triggers Hilt's code generation, and it also creates the application-level Hilt components.

Create the Application Class:

```
@HiltAndroidApp
class MyApplication : Application() {
    // Optional: Any global initialization
}
```

Declare the Application Class in AndroidManifest.xml:

Make sure to specify your application class in the AndroidManifest.xml.

```
<application
    android:name=".MyApplication"
    android:allowBackup="true"
    android:icon="@mipmap/ic_launcher"
    android:label="@string/app_name"
    android:roundIcon="@mipmap/ic_launcher_round"
    android:supportsRtl="true"
    android:theme="@style/Theme.AppCompat.Light.NoActionBar">
    ...
</application>
```

Step 3: Creating Modules for Dependency Provision

Modules are classes annotated with @Module that provide dependencies for Hilt. Use the @Provides annotation within the module to define methods that return instances of the required dependencies.

Create a Module:

```kotlin
@Module
@InstallIn(SingletonComponent::class) // Specify the component that uses this module
object NetworkModule {

    @Provides
    @Singleton // Scope to the entire application
    fun provideRetrofit(): Retrofit {
        return Retrofit.Builder()
            .baseUrl("https://api.example.com/")
            .addConverterFactory(GsonConverterFactory.create())
            .build()
    }

    @Provides
    @Singleton
    fun provideApiService(retrofit: Retrofit): ApiService {
        return retrofit.create(ApiService::class.java)
    }
}
```

In this example, NetworkModule provides instances of Retrofit and ApiService for the entire application.

Step 4: Injecting Dependencies into Activities and Fragments

With Hilt set up, you can easily inject dependencies into your Activities and Fragments using the @AndroidEntryPoint annotation. This annotation tells Hilt to provide the dependencies declared in the modules.

Injecting Dependencies in an Activity:

```kotlin
@AndroidEntryPoint
class MainActivity : AppCompatActivity() {

    @Inject // Use the inject annotation to get the dependency
    lateinit var apiService: ApiService

    override fun onCreate(savedInstanceState: Bundle?) {
        super.onCreate(savedInstanceState)
```

```
        setContentView(R.layout.activity_main)

        // Use the injected apiService
        fetchData()
    }

    private fun fetchData() {
        // Use apiService to make network requests
    }
}
```

Injecting Dependencies in a Fragment:

```
@AndroidEntryPoint
class UserFragment : Fragment() {

    @Inject
    lateinit var apiService: ApiService

    override fun onViewCreated(view: View, savedInstanceState: Bundle?) {
        super.onViewCreated(view, savedInstanceState)

        // Use the injected apiService
        loadUserData()
    }

    private fun loadUserData() {
        // Use apiService to load user data
    }
}
```

Step 5: Scoping Dependencies

Properly managing the lifecycle of your dependencies using scopes is crucial. Hilt provides built-in scopes like @Singleton, @ActivityScoped, and @FragmentScoped. You can define your own custom scopes if needed.

Creating a FragmentScoped Dependency:

```
@Module
```

```
@InstallIn(FragmentComponent::class)
object UserModule {

    @Provides
    @FragmentScoped
    fun provideUserViewModel(apiService: ApiService): UserViewModel {
        return UserViewModel(apiService)
    }
}
```

Injecting a Scoped Dependency in a Fragment:

```
@AndroidEntryPoint
class UserFragment : Fragment() {

    @Inject
    lateinit var userViewModel: UserViewModel

    override fun onViewCreated(view: View, savedInstanceState: Bundle?) {
        super.onViewCreated(view, savedInstanceState)

        // Use the injected userViewModel
        userViewModel.getUserData()
    }
}
```

Step 6: Testing with Hilt

Hilt makes it easier to write unit tests by allowing you to provide mock implementations for your dependencies.

Add Testing Dependencies:

In your build.gradle, include the necessary testing dependencies.

```
androidTestImplementation "com.google.dagger:hilt-android-testing:2.x"
kaptAndroidTest "com.google.dagger:hilt-compiler:2.x"
```

Creating a Test Module:

Create a test module that provides mock implementations of your dependencies.

```
@Module
@InstallIn(SingletonComponent::class)
object TestModule {

    @Provides
    @Singleton
    fun provideMockApiService(): ApiService {
        return MockApiService()
    }
}
```

Using Hilt in Tests:

Use Hilt's test support annotations to set up your tests.

```
@HiltAndroidTest
class MainActivityTest {

    @get:Rule
    var hiltRule = HiltAndroidRule(this)

    @Before
    fun init() {
        hiltRule.inject()
    }

    @Test
    fun testApiService() {
        // Write test cases using injected mockApiService
    }
}
```

Setting up Dagger and Hilt in your Android project streamlines the process of managing dependencies, ultimately leading to cleaner, more maintainable code. With Hilt's built-in annotations and automated dependency management, developers can easily inject dependencies into Activities, Fragments, and ViewModels without the complexity associated with traditional DI frameworks. By following the steps outlined in this section, you can effectively implement DI in your Android applications, enhancing both development speed and code quality. With the foundation of DI laid down, you can now focus on building powerful, modular Android applications that are easier to test and maintain.

6.3 Advanced Dagger Features: Multi-Binding and Modularization

Dagger is a powerful dependency injection framework that helps Android developers manage the complexities of dependency injection in a clean and efficient way. While basic dependency injection setup is often sufficient for simple applications, more complex scenarios benefit from advanced features like multi-binding and modularization. In this section, we will explore these advanced features in detail, demonstrating how they can enhance your application's architecture and improve code organization.

Multi-Binding in Dagger

Multi-binding allows you to bind multiple implementations of a particular type to a single key in Dagger. This feature is particularly useful when you want to provide different implementations of an interface, enabling you to easily switch between them at runtime or to compose behavior from multiple sources.

1. Using Multi-Binding

To use multi-binding, you need to follow these steps:

Define an Interface: Create an interface that will represent the type you want to bind multiple implementations for.

```
interface PaymentProcessor {
    fun processPayment(amount: Double)
}
```

Create Implementations: Define multiple implementations of this interface.

```
class CreditCardProcessor : PaymentProcessor {
    override fun processPayment(amount: Double) {
        // Logic for credit card payment
        println("Processed credit card payment of $amount")
```

```kotlin
    }
}

class PayPalProcessor : PaymentProcessor {
    override fun processPayment(amount: Double) {
        // Logic for PayPal payment
        println("Processed PayPal payment of $amount")
    }
}
```

Bind Implementations in a Module: Use the @IntoSet or @IntoMap annotations in a Dagger module to bind the implementations.

```kotlin
@Module
@InstallIn(SingletonComponent::class)
abstract class PaymentModule {

    @Binds
    @IntoSet
    abstract fun bindCreditCardProcessor(processor: CreditCardProcessor):
PaymentProcessor

    @Binds
    @IntoSet
    abstract fun bindPayPalProcessor(processor: PayPalProcessor): PaymentProcessor
}
```

Injecting Multi-Bound Dependencies: When you want to use the multi-bound dependencies, inject them as a Set<PaymentProcessor>.

```kotlin
class PaymentService @Inject constructor(private val processors:
Set<PaymentProcessor>) {
    fun processAllPayments(amount: Double) {
        processors.forEach { it.processPayment(amount) }
    }
}
```

2. Multi-Binding with Maps

In addition to sets, Dagger also supports multi-binding with maps, allowing you to associate keys with values.

Bind Implementations with Keys: Use the @IntoMap annotation along with a custom key annotation.

```
@Module
@InstallIn(SingletonComponent::class)
abstract class PaymentMapModule {

    @Binds
    @IntoMap
    @ProcessorKey("credit_card")
    abstract fun bindCreditCardProcessor(processor: CreditCardProcessor):
PaymentProcessor

    @Binds
    @IntoMap
    @ProcessorKey("paypal")
    abstract fun bindPayPalProcessor(processor: PayPalProcessor): PaymentProcessor
}

@MapKey
@Retention(AnnotationRetention.RUNTIME)
annotation class ProcessorKey(val value: String)
```

Injecting Map of Implementations: Inject the map in the consuming class.

```
class PaymentService @Inject constructor(private val processors: Map<String,
@JvmSuppressWildcards PaymentProcessor>) {
    fun processPayment(type: String, amount: Double) {
        processors[type]?.processPayment(amount) ?: println("No processor found for
$type")
    }
}
```

Modularization in Dagger

Modularization refers to breaking down a large application into smaller, self-contained modules. This not only improves the manageability and scalability of your application but also enhances build performance and encourages reusability. Dagger supports modularization, allowing you to create separate components and modules that can be independently tested and maintained.

1. Benefits of Modularization

- **Separation of Concerns**: Different modules can handle specific features or layers of your application, promoting cleaner code.
- **Independent Testing**: You can easily test individual modules without requiring the entire application.
- **Improved Build Times**: Smaller modules can reduce build times, especially in larger applications, as changes in one module don't require recompilation of the entire app.

2. Creating Modules

Define Separate Modules: Create separate Dagger modules for different features of your application. For example, you might have an AuthModule, NetworkModule, and UserModule.

```
@Module
@InstallIn(SingletonComponent::class)
object AuthModule {

  @Provides
  @Singleton
  fun provideAuthService(): AuthService {
    return AuthService()
  }
}

@Module
@InstallIn(ActivityComponent::class)
object UserModule {

  @Provides
  fun provideUserViewModel(authService: AuthService): UserViewModel {
    return UserViewModel(authService)
  }
}
```

Define Components: Create different Dagger components for your modules. This helps in controlling the visibility and scope of the dependencies.

```
@Component(modules = [NetworkModule::class])
interface AppComponent {
    fun inject(application: MyApplication)
}


@Component(modules = [UserModule::class])
interface ActivityComponent {
    fun inject(activity: MainActivity)
}
```

Using Component Dependencies: You can also make components depend on each other. This allows you to share dependencies across different parts of your application without duplication.

```
@Component(dependencies = [AppComponent::class])
interface MainActivityComponent {
    fun inject(activity: MainActivity)
}
```

3. Injecting Across Modules

When you have multiple modules, you can easily inject dependencies across them. For instance, if your UserViewModel requires a dependency from AuthModule, you can include it in the constructor.

```
class UserViewModel @Inject constructor(private val authService: AuthService) {
    // ViewModel logic
}
```

Best Practices for Multi-Binding and Modularization

- **Use Descriptive Names**: When using multi-binding with maps, choose descriptive keys to make it clear what each implementation does.
- **Keep Modules Focused**: Each module should have a clear responsibility to avoid bloating and making it harder to understand.

- **Limit Dependencies Between Modules**: Try to keep module dependencies to a minimum. This reduces coupling and makes your modules easier to manage.
- **Leverage Dagger's Scoping**: Use Dagger's scoping annotations to control the lifecycle of your dependencies, especially when working with modules.
- **Regularly Refactor**: As your application evolves, revisit your module structure and refactor to ensure optimal organization and maintainability.

Advanced Dagger features like multi-binding and modularization are invaluable tools for building scalable and maintainable Android applications. Multi-binding allows you to easily manage multiple implementations of a type, enabling flexibility and extensibility in your code. Meanwhile, modularization helps you break your application into manageable pieces, promoting separation of concerns and improving testability. By leveraging these features, you can create an organized codebase that is easier to maintain, extend, and test, ultimately leading to better software quality. With a firm understanding of these advanced concepts, you can elevate your Android development practices and create robust applications with Dagger.

Chapter 7: Working with Background Tasks: WorkManager and Coroutines

In this chapter, we will dive into the management of background tasks in Android using WorkManager and Kotlin Coroutines. You will learn the importance of executing tasks outside the main UI thread to ensure your applications remain responsive and efficient. We'll start by exploring WorkManager, the recommended solution for scheduling deferrable and guaranteed background work, discussing how to set up constraints, chaining tasks, and handling task failures gracefully. Next, we'll transition to Kotlin Coroutines, a powerful feature for asynchronous programming that allows you to write cleaner, more manageable code for handling concurrent operations. You'll learn how to launch coroutines, manage scopes, and utilize structured concurrency to execute background tasks in a way that enhances readability and maintainability. Through practical examples, we'll illustrate how to combine WorkManager and Coroutines effectively, enabling you to create applications that perform well under various conditions. By the end of this chapter, you will be equipped with the skills to implement robust background processing solutions that enhance user experience and application performance.

7.1 Mastering Coroutines for Asynchronous Processing

Asynchronous programming is an essential aspect of modern mobile application development. It allows apps to perform tasks like network requests, database operations, and other I/O operations without blocking the main thread, which can lead to a poor user experience. In the Android ecosystem, Kotlin Coroutines provide a powerful and flexible way to handle asynchronous programming, making it easier to write, read, and maintain code. This section will cover the fundamentals of Kotlin Coroutines, best practices for using them in Android applications, and practical examples to help you master asynchronous processing.

What are Coroutines?

Coroutines are lightweight, cooperative threads that can be suspended and resumed without blocking a thread. They enable developers to write asynchronous, non-blocking code in a sequential manner, making the code more readable and easier to follow.

Key Features of Coroutines:

- **Lightweight**: Unlike threads, coroutines are not tied to a specific thread and can run on any thread, allowing for efficient resource usage.
- **Structured Concurrency**: Coroutines provide a structured way to manage concurrent tasks, making it easier to handle cancellation and error propagation.
- **Easy to Read**: Coroutines allow developers to write asynchronous code that looks similar to synchronous code, enhancing readability.

Setting Up Coroutines in an Android Project

To start using coroutines in your Android project, you need to add the necessary dependencies.

Add Dependencies: Open your app-level build.gradle file and add the following dependencies:

```
dependencies {
    implementation "org.jetbrains.kotlinx:kotlinx-coroutines-core:1.x.x"
    implementation "org.jetbrains.kotlinx:kotlinx-coroutines-android:1.x.x"
}
```

Replace 1.x.x with the latest stable version available on Maven Central.

Enable Kotlin Plugin: Ensure that the Kotlin plugin is enabled in your project. If it's not already present, you can add it in the project-level build.gradle:

```
buildscript {
    ext.kotlin_version = '1.x.x'
    repositories {
        google()
        mavenCentral()
    }
    dependencies {
        classpath "org.jetbrains.kotlin:kotlin-gradle-plugin:$kotlin_version"
    }
}
```

Basic Coroutine Concepts

Before diving into practical examples, it's essential to understand some core concepts of coroutines.

Coroutine Scope: A coroutine scope defines the context in which coroutines run. Scopes manage the lifecycle of coroutines and ensure that they are properly cancelled when no longer needed.

- **GlobalScope**: A singleton scope that is used for launching top-level coroutines that are not tied to any job or lifecycle.
- **LifecycleScope**: A scope tied to an Android component's lifecycle (e.g., Activity, Fragment), which automatically cancels coroutines when the lifecycle owner is destroyed.

```
lifecycleScope.launch {
    // Coroutine code goes here
}
```

Dispatchers: Dispatchers determine the thread on which the coroutine will run. Common dispatchers include:

- **Dispatchers.Main**: Used for UI-related work on the main thread.
- **Dispatchers.IO**: Optimized for offloading blocking I/O tasks to a shared pool of threads.
- **Dispatchers.Default**: Used for CPU-intensive work.

```
// Launching a coroutine on the IO dispatcher
withContext(Dispatchers.IO) {
    // Perform I/O operations
}
```

Creating and Running Coroutines

Creating a coroutine is straightforward using the launch or async builder functions.

Launch: The launch builder is used for launching a new coroutine that does not return a result.

```
lifecycleScope.launch {
    // Coroutine work
}
```

Async: The async builder is used for launching a coroutine that returns a result, allowing you to use the await() function to retrieve the result.

```
val deferredResult = async {
    // Perform some computation
    return@async 42 // Returning a result
}
```

```
val result = deferredResult.await()
```

Error Handling in Coroutines

Handling errors in coroutines is essential for maintaining a smooth user experience. Coroutines provide structured error handling that propagates exceptions through coroutine hierarchies.

Try-Catch Blocks: You can wrap coroutine code in a try-catch block to handle exceptions.

```
lifecycleScope.launch {
    try {
        // Code that may throw an exception
    } catch (e: Exception) {
        // Handle the exception
    }
}
```

CoroutineExceptionHandler: You can create a CoroutineExceptionHandler to handle uncaught exceptions from coroutines.

```
val exceptionHandler = CoroutineExceptionHandler { _, exception ->
    println("Caught $exception")
}
```

```
lifecycleScope.launch(exceptionHandler) {
    // Coroutine code that may throw an exception
}
```

Cancellation of Coroutines

Coroutines can be cancelled, which is vital for preventing memory leaks and ensuring that tasks do not run longer than necessary.

Cancellation with Job: When you launch a coroutine, it is associated with a Job. You can cancel this job to cancel the coroutine.

```
val job = lifecycleScope.launch {
    // Coroutine work
}

// Cancel the coroutine
job.cancel()
```

Cooperative Cancellation: Coroutines are cancellable at suspension points. You should check for cancellation regularly in long-running operations using isActive.

```
withContext(Dispatchers.IO) {
    while (isActive) {
        // Perform work
    }
}
```

Using Coroutines with Android Components

Coroutines can be easily integrated with Android components like Activities, Fragments, and ViewModels. Here's how to use them effectively.

In ViewModel: Using coroutines in a ViewModel allows for long-running operations without blocking the UI.

```
class MyViewModel : ViewModel() {
    fun fetchData() {
        viewModelScope.launch {
            val data = withContext(Dispatchers.IO) {
                // Perform network call
            }
            // Update LiveData with fetched data
        }
    }
}
```

```
}
```

In Activities/Fragments: You can launch coroutines in the lifecycleScope of Activities or Fragments to perform asynchronous tasks.

```
class MyFragment : Fragment() {
    override fun onViewCreated(view: View, savedInstanceState: Bundle?) {
        super.onViewCreated(view, savedInstanceState)

        lifecycleScope.launch {
            val result = withContext(Dispatchers.IO) {
                // Fetch data
            }
            // Update UI with the result
        }
    }
}
```

Best Practices for Using Coroutines

- **Use Appropriate Scopes**: Always use lifecycleScope in Activities and Fragments, and viewModelScope in ViewModels to prevent memory leaks and manage coroutine lifecycles efficiently.
- **Prefer async for Concurrent Tasks**: Use async when you need to perform multiple concurrent operations and combine their results.
- **Handle Cancellation Properly**: Ensure your coroutines can be cancelled appropriately, especially during configuration changes or when the user navigates away from a screen.
- **Test Coroutines**: Use the runBlockingTest function from the kotlinx-coroutines-test library to test coroutine code in unit tests.

Mastering Kotlin Coroutines is essential for Android developers looking to create responsive and efficient applications. By understanding the concepts of coroutines, setting them up correctly, and utilizing best practices, you can effectively manage asynchronous tasks in your apps. Coroutines enhance code readability and maintainability, enabling you to focus on building robust features without being bogged down by the complexities of traditional asynchronous programming. As you continue to explore the power of coroutines, you'll find that they are an indispensable tool in your Android development toolkit.

7.2 Implementing Background Tasks with WorkManager

Background tasks are essential in modern mobile applications, enabling developers to perform long-running operations without affecting the user experience. With Android's evolving architecture, the WorkManager API has emerged as the go-to solution for managing background work that needs guaranteed execution, even if the app is killed or the device restarts. In this section, we'll explore the WorkManager in detail, including its setup, key components, and practical implementation techniques for background task management.

What is WorkManager?

WorkManager is part of Android Jetpack and provides a flexible and robust framework for scheduling and executing background tasks. It is particularly useful for:

- **Deferring work**: Tasks that don't need to execute immediately.
- **Constraints**: Running tasks under specific conditions, such as network connectivity or device charging state.
- **Guaranteed execution**: Ensuring that tasks are executed even if the app is not currently running.

WorkManager abstracts away the complexities of background task execution, choosing the most appropriate threading mechanism based on the task's requirements and system constraints.

Key Features of WorkManager

- **Task Constraints**: Specify conditions under which a task should run, such as requiring network connectivity or charging state.
- **Chaining Work**: Combine multiple tasks and set dependencies between them.
- **Back-off Policies**: Define how to handle failures with policies like exponential backoff.
- **Flexible Scheduling**: Work can be scheduled to run immediately or at a later time, or periodically.
- **Compatibility**: Works on all Android devices, regardless of API level.

Setting Up WorkManager

To use WorkManager in your Android project, follow these steps:

Add Dependencies: Open your app-level build.gradle file and add the following dependency:

```
dependencies {
    implementation "androidx.work:work-runtime-ktx:2.x.x" // Use the latest version
}
```

Sync Your Project: Sync your Gradle files to download the WorkManager library.

Creating a Worker

A Worker is the main component of WorkManager that performs the background task. Here's how to create a simple Worker:

Define Your Worker: Create a class that extends Worker and override the doWork() method.

```
class MyWorker(appContext: Context, workerParams: WorkerParameters) :
Worker(appContext, workerParams) {
    override fun doWork(): Result {
        // Perform the background task here
        try {
            // Simulate a long-running task (e.g., network call)
            Thread.sleep(2000) // Example: Sleep for 2 seconds
            // Return success
            return Result.success()
        } catch (e: Exception) {
            // Log error and return failure
            return Result.failure()
        }
    }
}
```

Specify Input and Output Data: You can pass data into the Worker and retrieve data upon completion using Data.

```
val inputData = Data.Builder()
    .putString("key", "value")
    .build()
```

```kotlin
class MyWorker(appContext: Context, workerParams: WorkerParameters) :
Worker(appContext, workerParams) {
    override fun doWork(): Result {
        val inputValue = inputData.getString("key")
        // Process inputValue...
        return Result.success(Data.Builder().putString("resultKey", "resultValue").build())
    }
}
```

Enqueuing Work

Once you have defined your Worker, you can schedule it using the WorkManager:

Create a WorkRequest: Define a OneTimeWorkRequest or PeriodicWorkRequest.

```kotlin
val workRequest = OneTimeWorkRequestBuilder<MyWorker>()
    .setInputData(inputData)
    .build()
```

Enqueue the WorkRequest: Use WorkManager to enqueue the work.

```kotlin
WorkManager.getInstance(context).enqueue(workRequest)
```

Using Constraints

You can specify constraints for your Worker to control when it runs. For example, you can set constraints for network connectivity or device charging state.

```kotlin
val constraints = Constraints.Builder()
    .setRequiredNetworkType(NetworkType.CONNECTED) // Requires network connectivity
    .setRequiresCharging(true) // Requires device to be charging
    .build()
```

```kotlin
val workRequest = OneTimeWorkRequestBuilder<MyWorker>()
    .setConstraints(constraints)
    .build()
```

Chaining Work

WorkManager allows you to chain multiple Workers, enabling complex workflows where one task depends on the completion of another.

Creating Chained Work: You can use the beginWith() and then() methods to chain Workers.

```
val firstWork = OneTimeWorkRequestBuilder<FirstWorker>().build()
val secondWork = OneTimeWorkRequestBuilder<SecondWorker>().build()

WorkManager.getInstance(context)
  .beginWith(firstWork)
  .then(secondWork)
  .enqueue()
```

Handling Results Between Workers: You can pass results from one Worker to another using output data.

```
class FirstWorker(appContext: Context, workerParams: WorkerParameters) :
Worker(appContext, workerParams) {
   override fun doWork(): Result {
     // Do some work...
     val outputData = Data.Builder().putString("output", "result").build()
     return Result.success(outputData)
   }
}

class SecondWorker(appContext: Context, workerParams: WorkerParameters) :
Worker(appContext, workerParams) {
   override fun doWork(): Result {
     val inputData = inputData.getString("output") // Retrieve output from FirstWorker
     // Do something with inputData...
     return Result.success()
   }
}
```

Back-off Policies

When a Worker fails, you can configure a back-off policy that determines when to retry the task.

Using Back-off Policies: You can specify the initial delay and back-off criteria.

```
val workRequest = OneTimeWorkRequestBuilder<MyWorker>()
  .setBackoffCriteria(
     BackoffPolicy.EXPONENTIAL,
     OneTimeWorkRequest.MIN_BACKOFF_MILLIS,
     TimeUnit.MILLISECONDS
  )
  .build()
```

Observing Work Status

You can observe the status of your work using LiveData or by querying the WorkManager.

Using LiveData: WorkManager provides LiveData objects that you can observe for changes in the status of your WorkRequest.

```
val workInfoLiveData =
WorkManager.getInstance(context).getWorkInfoByIdLiveData(workRequest.id)

workInfoLiveData.observe(this, Observer { workInfo ->
  if (workInfo != null && workInfo.state.isFinished) {
     // Work is finished
  }
})
```
Querying Work: You can query the status of a work request using its ID.
kotlin
Copy code
```
WorkManager.getInstance(context).getWorkInfoById(workRequest.id).observe(this,
Observer { workInfo ->
  // Process workInfo
})
```

Cancelling Work

If necessary, you can cancel work requests that have been scheduled.

Canceling a Work Request: Use the cancelWorkById() method to cancel a specific work request.

WorkManager.getInstance(context).cancelWorkById(workRequest.id)

Canceling All Work Requests: To cancel all work of a specific type, you can use:

WorkManager.getInstance(context).cancelAllWorkByTag("myWorkTag")

Best Practices for Using WorkManager

- **Use Unique Work Names**: Assign unique names or tags to your work requests to prevent conflicts and manage them effectively.
- **Monitor Work Status**: Implement monitoring of work status to handle success and failure cases appropriately.
- **Leverage Constraints**: Use constraints to ensure that work runs only under the right conditions, conserving resources and improving efficiency.
- **Use Chaining Wisely**: Chain work requests when tasks depend on each other, but avoid creating overly complex chains that can be difficult to manage.
- **Test Background Tasks**: Use the Android Testing Support Library to test your background tasks and ensure they function as expected.

WorkManager provides a powerful and flexible solution for managing background tasks in Android applications. Its ability to handle task scheduling, constraints, and guaranteed execution makes it an indispensable tool for developers. By mastering WorkManager, you can ensure that your app performs long-running operations efficiently and reliably, enhancing the overall user experience. With the ability to create complex workflows, monitor task status, and leverage built-in error handling, WorkManager empowers you to build robust and responsive applications that meet the demands of modern mobile development.

7.3 Optimizing Battery and Resource Usage for Background Work

As mobile applications continue to evolve and incorporate more features, optimizing battery life and resource usage has become a critical aspect of Android development. Users expect apps to run efficiently without draining their device's battery or consuming excessive system resources. This section focuses on best practices and strategies to optimize battery and resource usage when implementing background work with WorkManager.

Understanding Battery Consumption and Resource Usage

When performing background tasks, it's essential to be aware of how certain operations can impact battery life and resource usage. Background tasks can consume battery power due to:

- **Network Requests**: Frequent or unnecessary network calls can quickly drain battery life, especially if they occur when the device is not connected to Wi-Fi.
- **CPU Usage**: High CPU activity, such as intensive calculations or continuous processing, can lead to increased power consumption.
- **Disk I/O Operations**: Writing and reading large amounts of data from disk can impact performance and battery life.

To optimize battery and resource usage, developers must implement strategies that minimize unnecessary activity and leverage system features intelligently.

Strategies for Optimizing Background Work

Here are some best practices to optimize battery and resource usage while using WorkManager for background tasks:

Use Constraints Wisely

Constraints allow you to specify conditions under which your background tasks should run. By ensuring that tasks only execute when necessary, you can significantly reduce battery consumption.

Network Constraints: Specify that work should only run when connected to Wi-Fi instead of cellular data to avoid draining the battery.

```
val constraints = Constraints.Builder()
    .setRequiredNetworkType(NetworkType.CONNECTED) // Only run if connected to Wi-Fi
    .setRequiresBatteryNotLow(true) // Ensure battery is not low
    .build()
```

Charging Constraints: Use the charging constraint to execute heavy tasks only when the device is plugged in.

```
val constraints = Constraints.Builder()
```

```
.setRequiresCharging(true) // Run only when charging
.build()
```

Batch Network Requests

Instead of making multiple network requests throughout the day, consider batching requests together into a single background task. This reduces the frequency of network calls and optimizes battery usage.

Combining Requests: Gather data that can be processed together and send it in a single request.

```
class BatchDataWorker(appContext: Context, workerParams: WorkerParameters) :
Worker(appContext, workerParams) {
    override fun doWork(): Result {
        // Collect and send batched data to the server
        return Result.success()
    }
}
```

Utilize Exponential Backoff for Failed Tasks

When a background task fails, instead of retrying immediately, use an exponential backoff strategy. This means that the next attempt will be delayed, thus reducing resource usage and preventing rapid battery drain.

```
val workRequest = OneTimeWorkRequestBuilder<MyWorker>()
    .setBackoffCriteria(
        BackoffPolicy.EXPONENTIAL,
        OneTimeWorkRequest.MIN_BACKOFF_MILLIS,
        TimeUnit.MILLISECONDS
    )
    .build()
```

Schedule Work During Idle Times

Leverage the system's ability to schedule tasks during idle times or when the device is connected to power and Wi-Fi. You can use setRequiresDeviceIdle(true) as part of your constraints to ensure that tasks run only when the device is idle.

```
val constraints = Constraints.Builder()
    .setRequiresDeviceIdle(true) // Run only when the device is idle
    .build()
```

Reduce Frequency of Periodic Work

If you're using PeriodicWorkRequest, carefully consider the frequency of background tasks. The default minimum interval is 15 minutes, which should be adhered to, but keep in mind that running tasks more frequently than necessary can waste resources.

```
val periodicWorkRequest = PeriodicWorkRequestBuilder<MyWorker>(15,
TimeUnit.MINUTES)
    .setConstraints(constraints)
    .build()
```

Avoid Long-Running Tasks on the Main Thread

Ensure that all heavy processing, such as file I/O or CPU-intensive calculations, is performed on a background thread. Use WorkManager to run such tasks instead of blocking the main thread, which can lead to a poor user experience and increased battery consumption.

```
class MyWorker(appContext: Context, workerParams: WorkerParameters) :
Worker(appContext, workerParams) {
    override fun doWork(): Result {
        // Perform long-running task on a background thread
        return Result.success()
    }
}
```

Monitoring and Testing Battery Usage

To ensure that your background work optimizations are effective, it is vital to monitor and test your application's battery usage during development:

Android Profiler: Use the Android Profiler in Android Studio to monitor CPU, memory, and network usage while running background tasks. This tool helps identify bottlenecks and high resource consumption points.

Battery Historian: Use Battery Historian to analyze battery usage over time and check how your app impacts battery life. This tool provides detailed insights into battery consumption patterns.

Testing on Real Devices: Always test your app on real devices under various conditions (e.g., low battery, device idle) to understand how background tasks affect performance and battery life.

Optimizing battery and resource usage for background work in Android applications is crucial for maintaining a good user experience and extending device battery life. By following best practices such as using constraints, batching requests, and monitoring resource usage, developers can ensure that their applications run efficiently in the background. WorkManager provides a robust framework for managing background tasks while offering developers the flexibility to optimize their applications for battery and resource consumption. By implementing these strategies, you can create applications that not only perform well but also respect users' device resources and enhance overall satisfaction.

Chapter 8: Enhanced User Experience with Animations and Transitions

In this chapter, we will explore the vital role of animations and transitions in creating engaging and interactive user experiences in Android applications. You will learn how to implement various animation techniques using the Animation and Animator APIs, as well as the powerful MotionLayout for more complex animations. We'll discuss how to apply property animations, view transitions, and drawable animations to enhance the visual appeal of your app and improve user interactions. Additionally, we'll cover best practices for designing smooth and meaningful animations that contribute to the overall usability of your app, ensuring that they are not only visually appealing but also intuitive. You will also discover how to manage animation states and performance considerations to keep your application responsive. By the end of this chapter, you will have the skills to create dynamic, captivating UIs that not only grab users' attention but also guide them seamlessly through your app, ultimately enhancing their overall experience.

8.1 Working with Property Animations and Custom Interpolators

In modern Android development, creating engaging and visually appealing user interfaces is essential for enhancing the user experience. Property animations are a powerful way to add life to your apps by smoothly transitioning UI elements between states. This section explores the fundamentals of property animations, how to implement them in your Android application, and the creation of custom interpolators for more tailored animation effects.

Understanding Property Animations

Property animations allow you to animate the properties of objects in your application, such as views, layout parameters, and drawable properties. Unlike the older view animations, property animations provide a more flexible and powerful way to achieve smooth transitions. They are capable of animating any property of an object that has a getter and setter, making them versatile for various UI components.

The key classes for property animations in Android are:

ObjectAnimator: This class animates a specific property of an object (such as a View) from one value to another over a specified duration.

ValueAnimator: This class is used to animate between values over time without directly manipulating a specific object's property. It provides a value update callback that can be used to change properties manually.

AnimatorSet: This class allows you to play multiple animations together or in sequence, enabling more complex animations.

Implementing Property Animations

To implement property animations, follow these steps:

Animating with ObjectAnimator

The simplest way to create an animation is by using ObjectAnimator. For example, you can animate the translationX property of a View to move it across the screen.

```
// Create an ObjectAnimator to animate translationX
val animator = ObjectAnimator.ofFloat(view, "translationX", 0f, 500f)
animator.duration = 1000 // Duration in milliseconds
animator.start() // Start the animation
```

In this example, the view will move from its original position to 500 pixels to the right over one second.

Using ValueAnimator for Custom Animations

ValueAnimator provides greater control and flexibility for animations. It doesn't directly manipulate a property; instead, you can define a range of values that you want to animate between.

```
val valueAnimator = ValueAnimator.ofFloat(0f, 1f)
valueAnimator.duration = 1000 // Duration in milliseconds

valueAnimator.addUpdateListener { animation ->
    val animatedValue = animation.animatedValue as Float
    view.alpha = animatedValue // Change alpha from 0 to 1
}

valueAnimator.start() // Start the animation
```

In this example, the alpha property of the view is animated from 0 (completely transparent) to 1 (fully opaque) over one second.

Animating Multiple Properties with AnimatorSet

To animate multiple properties together, use AnimatorSet. You can define the timing for each animation to play simultaneously or sequentially.

```
val translationXAnimator = ObjectAnimator.ofFloat(view, "translationX", 0f, 500f)
val alphaAnimator = ObjectAnimator.ofFloat(view, "alpha", 0f, 1f)

val animatorSet = AnimatorSet()
animatorSet.playTogether(translationXAnimator, alphaAnimator)
animatorSet.duration = 1000 // Duration for the entire set
animatorSet.start() // Start the animations
```

This will animate both the translation and alpha properties simultaneously.

Custom Interpolators

Interpolators define the rate of change of an animation, allowing you to create various effects, such as acceleration, deceleration, or bounciness. Android provides several built-in interpolators, but you can create custom interpolators to suit your specific animation needs.

Using Built-in Interpolators

You can easily apply built-in interpolators such as AccelerateDecelerateInterpolator, BounceInterpolator, and LinearInterpolator by setting them on your animator.

```
animator.interpolator = AccelerateDecelerateInterpolator()
```

Creating a Custom Interpolator

To create a custom interpolator, you need to implement the TimeInterpolator interface and override the getInterpolation() method. This method receives a value between 0 and 1, representing the progress of the animation.

Here's an example of a simple custom interpolator that creates a bouncing effect:

```
class BounceInterpolator : TimeInterpolator {
    override fun getInterpolation(input: Float): Float {
        return if (input < 0.5) {
            2.0f * input * input // Accelerate
        } else {
            val bounceInput = input - 0.5f
            0.5f * (1 - bounceInput * bounceInput + 0.5f) // Decelerate with bounce
        }
    }
}
```

To use your custom interpolator in an animation:

```
val animator = ObjectAnimator.ofFloat(view, "translationY", 0f, 100f)
animator.interpolator = BounceInterpolator()
animator.duration = 1000
animator.start()
```

Tips for Effective Animations

Keep Animations Short: Long animations can frustrate users. Generally, animations should last between 200 to 500 milliseconds.

Ease In and Out: Use interpolators to create smooth transitions. Ease-in and ease-out effects make animations feel more natural.

Consider Performance: Heavy animations can affect performance. Use GPU-accelerated animations when possible by applying them to the properties of views that can be rendered directly (like translation, scale, and alpha).

Test on Multiple Devices: Different devices may have varying performance characteristics. Test animations on a range of devices to ensure smooth playback.

Avoid Overusing Animations: While animations enhance UI, overusing them can lead to a cluttered and confusing experience. Use them judiciously to draw attention to key elements.

Property animations, combined with custom interpolators, provide powerful tools for creating engaging and dynamic user interfaces in Android applications. By understanding the fundamentals of ObjectAnimator, ValueAnimator, and AnimatorSet, you can bring your app's UI to life. Additionally, creating custom interpolators allows you to fine-tune animations to achieve the desired visual effects. By following best practices, you can ensure that your animations enhance the user experience while maintaining performance and responsiveness.

8.2 Applying Transitions Between Activities and Fragments

Creating smooth transitions between activities and fragments is vital for delivering a polished user experience in Android applications. Transitions help users understand the flow of your app and enhance visual continuity. In this section, we will explore how to implement activity and fragment transitions effectively using Android's built-in transition framework, along with best practices for achieving seamless animations.

Understanding Transitions

Transitions are animations that occur when the user navigates between different parts of an app, such as switching from one activity to another or changing fragments within an activity. They provide visual feedback and improve the user's understanding of how the UI components relate to one another.

Android provides several built-in transitions, such as fade, slide, and explode, which can be easily applied to activities and fragments. In addition to built-in transitions, developers can create custom transitions to tailor animations to the app's specific design and flow.

Activity Transitions

To implement transitions between activities, follow these steps:

Defining Activity Transitions

You can define transitions in XML using the res/transition directory, or programmatically in your activity. For instance, here's how to create a simple fade transition using XML:

```xml
<!-- res/transition/fade_in.xml -->
<fade xmlns:android="http://schemas.android.com/apk/res/android"
   android:duration="300" />
```
xml
Copy code

```
<!-- res/transition/fade_out.xml -->
<fade xmlns:android="http://schemas.android.com/apk/res/android"
    android:duration="300" />
```

Applying Transitions in Activities

Once you've defined your transitions, you can apply them when starting a new activity. Here's an example of how to use these transitions:

```
val intent = Intent(this, SecondActivity::class.java)
startActivity(intent)
overridePendingTransition(R.transition.fade_in, R.transition.fade_out)
```

In this code, fade_in is applied when the new activity is launched, and fade_out is used for the current activity.

Using Built-in Transitions

Android also provides built-in transitions for simpler implementations. For example, you can use ActivityOptionsCompat to apply shared element transitions:

```
val options = ActivityOptionsCompat.makeSceneTransitionAnimation(this,
sharedElement, "transitionName")
startActivity(intent, options.toBundle())
```

Fragment Transitions

Fragment transitions can be applied similarly, allowing for smooth animations when adding, replacing, or removing fragments. The steps to achieve this include:

Setting Up Fragment Transitions

Define transitions in XML as you did for activities. Here's an example of a slide transition:

```
<!-- res/transition/slide_in.xml -->
<slide xmlns:android="http://schemas.android.com/apk/res/android"
    android:duration="300"
    android:slideEdge="start" />
```

```
<!-- res/transition/slide_out.xml -->
```

```xml
<slide xmlns:android="http://schemas.android.com/apk/res/android"
    android:duration="300"
    android:slideEdge="end" />
```

Applying Transitions to Fragments

When you perform fragment transactions, you can specify animations for entering and exiting fragments. Here's an example of how to use these transitions:

```kotlin
val fragment = MyFragment()
fragment.enterTransition =
TransitionInflater.from(context).inflateTransition(R.transition.slide_in)
fragment.exitTransition =
TransitionInflater.from(context).inflateTransition(R.transition.slide_out)

val transaction = supportFragmentManager.beginTransaction()
transaction.replace(R.id.fragment_container, fragment)
transaction.addToBackStack(null)
transaction.commit()
```

Using Fragment Animations with TransitionManager

You can also manage transitions more dynamically using TransitionManager. This approach is particularly useful when you want to animate changes in a ViewGroup containing fragments.

```kotlin
TransitionManager.beginDelayedTransition(fragmentContainer, Slide())
transaction.replace(R.id.fragment_container, fragment)
transaction.commit()
```

Best Practices for Transitions

Consistency in Animation Style

Ensure that transitions across activities and fragments follow a consistent style. This includes duration, type of animation (fade, slide, etc.), and overall visual aesthetics. Consistency enhances the user experience and keeps the app feeling cohesive.

Keep It Simple

Avoid overly complex animations that could distract users or hinder their navigation experience. Simple, subtle transitions are often more effective than elaborate ones.

Consider Performance

Heavy or long-running animations can negatively impact performance and user experience. Test transitions on various devices to ensure they run smoothly.

Leverage Shared Element Transitions

Use shared element transitions to create a sense of continuity when moving between activities or fragments. This technique enhances user engagement by visually connecting elements across screens.

Use TransitionListener

Consider using a TransitionListener to handle specific events during the transition process. This allows you to trigger actions when the transition starts or ends, improving user feedback and interaction.

```
val transition = Fade()
transition.addListener(object : Transition.TransitionListener {
    override fun onTransitionStart(transition: Transition) {
        // Code to run when the transition starts
    }

    override fun onTransitionEnd(transition: Transition) {
        // Code to run when the transition ends
    }

    override fun onTransitionCancel(transition: Transition) {}
    override fun onTransitionPause(transition: Transition) {}
    override fun onTransitionResume(transition: Transition) {}
})
```

Transitions between activities and fragments play a vital role in enhancing the user experience in Android applications. By implementing smooth animations, developers can create a more engaging and visually appealing app. Leveraging both built-in transitions and custom XML-defined animations, along with best practices, ensures that transitions are not only beautiful but also functional and efficient. By carefully designing these transitions, you can significantly improve the perceived performance and usability of your application.

8.3 Using MotionLayout for Complex Animations and Dynamic UIs

MotionLayout, part of the ConstraintLayout library, provides a powerful toolset for creating complex animations and transitions within your Android applications. It allows developers to animate views in a more intuitive way by defining motion scenes, creating visually rich experiences, and easily managing dynamic UIs. This section explores how to leverage MotionLayout for sophisticated animations, outlines its key components, and offers practical implementation examples.

Understanding MotionLayout

MotionLayout is designed to help developers create animations and transitions that go beyond simple view properties. It combines layout and animation capabilities, allowing for more flexible and intricate motion designs. Here are some key features:

Animation and Layout Together: MotionLayout enables you to define both layout properties and animations within a single XML file, allowing for seamless transitions between different states.

KeyFrames: You can define various key frames at different points in your animation timeline. This allows for precise control over how views behave during animations.

State Management: MotionLayout manages multiple states, enabling transitions between them. States can represent different layouts or configurations, and you can define how to animate between them.

Setting Up MotionLayout

To get started with MotionLayout, you first need to include the necessary dependencies in your build.gradle file:

```
dependencies {
    implementation "androidx.constraintlayout:constraintlayout:2.0.4"
}
```

After that, you can create a layout using MotionLayout in your XML file:

```xml
<androidx.constraintlayout.motion.widget.MotionLayout
    xmlns:android="http://schemas.android.com/apk/res/android"
    xmlns:app="http://schemas.android.com/apk/res-auto"
    android:id="@+id/motionLayout"
    android:layout_width="match_parent"
    android:layout_height="match_parent"
    app:layoutDescription="@xml/motion_scene">

    <ImageView
        android:id="@+id/imageView"
        android:layout_width="100dp"
        android:layout_height="100dp"
        android:src="@drawable/sample_image"
        app:layout_constraintBottom_toBottomOf="parent"
        app:layout_constraintEnd_toEndOf="parent"
        app:layout_constraintStart_toStartOf="parent"
        app:layout_constraintTop_toTopOf="parent" />

</androidx.constraintlayout.motion.widget.MotionLayout>
```

The layoutDescription attribute points to an XML file defining the motion scene, where you'll specify the transitions and states.

Defining Motion Scenes

A motion scene is an XML file where you define the animation states and transitions. Create a new XML file in the res/xml directory, for example, motion_scene.xml:

```xml
<MotionScene xmlns:android="http://schemas.android.com/apk/res/android"
    xmlns:app="http://schemas.android.com/apk/res-auto">

    <Transition
        app:constraintSetStart="@id/start"
        app:constraintSetEnd="@id/end"
        app:duration="500">
        <KeyFrame
            app:targetId="@id/imageView"
```

```
        app:framePosition="50"
        app:motionProgress="0.5"
        app:rotation="180"/>
  </Transition>

  <ConstraintSet android:id="@+id/start">
    <Constraint
      android:id="@id/imageView"
      app:layout_constraintBottom_toBottomOf="parent"
      app:layout_constraintEnd_toEndOf="parent"
      app:layout_constraintStart_toStartOf="parent"
      app:layout_constraintTop_toTopOf="parent" />
  </ConstraintSet>

  <ConstraintSet android:id="@+id/end">
    <Constraint
      android:id="@id/imageView"
      app:layout_constraintBottom_toTopOf="parent"
      app:layout_constraintEnd_toStartOf="parent"
      app:layout_constraintStart_toEndOf="parent"
      app:layout_constraintTop_toBottomOf="parent" />
  </ConstraintSet>
</MotionScene>
```

In this example, the Transition element defines how the ImageView moves from the start constraint set to the end constraint set over 500 milliseconds. The KeyFrame allows for additional adjustments at specific points during the transition.

Triggering Motion Layout Animations

To start a transition programmatically, you can call the transitionToEnd() or transitionToStart() methods from your MotionLayout instance:

```
val motionLayout = findViewById<MotionLayout>(R.id.motionLayout)

// Trigger the transition to the end state
motionLayout.transitionToEnd()
```

You can also set up triggers based on user interactions. For instance, you might trigger a transition when a button is clicked:

```
<Button
    android:id="@+id/button"
    android:layout_width="wrap_content"
    android:layout_height="wrap_content"
    android:text="Start Animation"
    app:layout_constraintBottom_toBottomOf="parent"
    app:layout_constraintEnd_toEndOf="parent"
    app:layout_constraintStart_toStartOf="parent"
    app:layout_constraintTop_toTopOf="parent"/>
```

In your activity or fragment:

```
val button = findViewById<Button>(R.id.button)
button.setOnClickListener {
    motionLayout.transitionToEnd()
}
```

KeyFrame Animation

KeyFrames in MotionLayout allow for detailed control of animations at specific points. You can define multiple keyframes in a transition to create dynamic animations. For instance, you can adjust the size, rotation, and alpha properties:

```
<KeyFrame
    app:targetId="@id/imageView"
    app:framePosition="25"
    app:scaleX="1.5"
    app:scaleY="1.5"/>
<KeyFrame
    app:targetId="@id/imageView"
    app:framePosition="75"
    app:alpha="0.5"/>
```

In this example, at 25% of the animation's duration, the ImageView scales up by 1.5 times, and at 75%, it fades to 50% opacity.

Using MotionLayout with Dynamic UIs

MotionLayout is particularly effective for creating responsive, dynamic UIs. You can leverage its capabilities to react to user interactions, orientation changes, or other events dynamically.

Responsive Design: You can define different motion scenes for different screen sizes or orientations, allowing for a responsive user experience. Simply create separate motion scene files for each configuration.

Listening to Transition Events: You can set up listeners to handle events during transitions. This enables you to trigger other actions when the transition starts or ends.

```
motionLayout.setTransitionListener(object : MotionLayout.TransitionListener {
    override fun onTransitionStart(motionLayout: MotionLayout, transitionId: Int) {
        // Code to run when the transition starts
    }

    override fun onTransitionEnd(motionLayout: MotionLayout, transitionId: Int) {
        // Code to run when the transition ends
    }

    override fun onTransitionCancel(motionLayout: MotionLayout, transitionId: Int) {}
    override fun onTransitionPause(motionLayout: MotionLayout, transitionId: Int) {}
    override fun onTransitionResume(motionLayout: MotionLayout, transitionId: Int) {}
})
```

Complex Interactions: MotionLayout allows for more complex user interactions. For example, you can define swipe gestures or dragging to create custom animations that respond to user input.

MotionLayout is a powerful tool for creating complex animations and dynamic UIs in Android applications. By combining layout definitions and animations in a single framework, developers can create engaging user experiences with relative ease. With features like keyframes, state management, and support for dynamic interactions, MotionLayout offers unparalleled flexibility for crafting intricate animations that respond to user actions. By embracing MotionLayout, you can enhance your app's visual appeal and provide users with an immersive experience that keeps them engaged.

Chapter 9: Security and Data Protection in Android Apps

In this chapter, we will focus on implementing robust security measures and data protection strategies in your Android applications. As security threats continue to evolve, it's essential to understand how to safeguard sensitive user information and ensure secure communications. We will begin by exploring the Android Keystore system, which allows you to securely store cryptographic keys and perform operations without exposing them. You will learn how to implement encryption techniques to protect data at rest and in transit, using libraries such as Jetpack Security and best practices for handling sensitive information. Additionally, we will discuss biometric authentication methods, including fingerprint and face recognition, to enhance user verification and improve app security. We'll also cover secure networking practices, including the use of HTTPS, certificate pinning, and validating user input to prevent common vulnerabilities. By the end of this chapter, you will have a comprehensive understanding of how to implement security best practices in your Android apps, ensuring user data is protected and instilling trust in your application.

9.1 Encrypting Data with Jetpack Security and Android Keystore

In today's digital landscape, securing sensitive user data is paramount for any mobile application. Android provides robust mechanisms for encryption, and two of the primary tools for safeguarding data are Jetpack Security and the Android Keystore system. This chapter will delve into these tools, exploring their capabilities and how to implement them effectively to protect sensitive information in your Android applications.

Understanding the Need for Data Encryption

Data encryption transforms readable data (plaintext) into an unreadable format (ciphertext) to prevent unauthorized access. This is especially crucial for mobile applications that often handle sensitive information, such as user credentials, financial details, and personal data. By encrypting data, developers can ensure that even if an attacker gains access to the device or the application's storage, they cannot easily read or misuse the sensitive information.

Jetpack Security Library

The Jetpack Security library simplifies the process of implementing secure data storage and handling sensitive data in Android applications. It provides a high-level API that abstracts the complexities of encryption and allows developers to focus on building their applications. Here are some key features of the Jetpack Security library:

Encryption and Decryption: Jetpack Security allows developers to easily encrypt and decrypt data using strong encryption algorithms without needing to manage the underlying cryptographic operations directly.

Shared Preferences Encryption: It can encrypt SharedPreferences, ensuring that sensitive user preferences are stored securely.

Integration with Android Keystore: Jetpack Security seamlessly integrates with the Android Keystore, which provides a secure way to store cryptographic keys.

Setting Up Jetpack Security

To get started with Jetpack Security, add the following dependency to your app's build.gradle file:

```
dependencies {
    implementation "androidx.security:security-crypto:1.1.0-alpha03"
}
```

Once you have added the dependency, you can start using Jetpack Security in your application.

Using Jetpack Security for Data Encryption

Encrypting Data: To encrypt data, you can use the EncryptedSharedPreferences class, which automatically handles the encryption of data stored in SharedPreferences. Here's how to set it up:

```
val masterKeyAlias = MasterKey.Builder(context)
    .setKeyScheme(MasterKey.KeyScheme.AES256_GCM)
    .setUserAuthenticationRequired(false)
    .build()

val sharedPreferences = EncryptedSharedPreferences.create(
```

```
  context,
  "secure_prefs",
  masterKeyAlias,
  EncryptedSharedPreferences.PrefKeyEncryptionScheme.AES256_SIV,
  EncryptedSharedPreferences.PrefValueEncryptionScheme.AES256_GCM
)

// To store data securely
with(sharedPreferences.edit()) {
  putString("user_email", "user@example.com")
  apply()
}
```

In this code, we create a master key using the MasterKey class. This key is used to encrypt and decrypt the SharedPreferences.

Decrypting Data: To retrieve the encrypted data, simply access it like you would with standard SharedPreferences:

```
val email = sharedPreferences.getString("user_email", null)
```

Jetpack Security automatically handles the decryption process, so you receive the plaintext value directly.

Android Keystore System

The Android Keystore system provides a secure container for cryptographic keys, allowing you to store and use keys without exposing them to the application's environment. This is crucial for key management, as it mitigates the risk of key extraction and unauthorized access.

Creating a Key Pair: To create a key pair in the Android Keystore, use the following code:

```
val keyPairGenerator =
KeyPairGenerator.getInstance(KeyProperties.KEY_ALGORITHM_RSA,
"AndroidKeyStore")
val keyGenParameterSpec = KeyGenParameterSpec.Builder(
  "my_key_alias",
  KeyProperties.PURPOSE_ENCRYPT or KeyProperties.PURPOSE_DECRYPT
```

```
)
    .setKeySize(2048)
    .setEncryptionPaddings(KeyProperties.ENCRYPTION_PADDING_RSA_OAEP)
    .build()

keyPairGenerator.initialize(keyGenParameterSpec)
val keyPair = keyPairGenerator.generateKeyPair()
```

In this code, we create an RSA key pair with the alias "my_key_alias" and specify that it will be used for both encryption and decryption.

Encrypting Data with a Key from the Keystore: After generating a key, you can use it to encrypt data:

```
val cipher = Cipher.getInstance("RSA/ECB/OAEPWithSHA-256AndMGF1Padding")
cipher.init(Cipher.ENCRYPT_MODE, keyPair.public)

val plaintext = "Sensitive Data".toByteArray()
val encryptedData = cipher.doFinal(plaintext)
```

Decrypting Data: Similarly, you can decrypt the data using the private key stored in the Keystore:

```
cipher.init(Cipher.DECRYPT_MODE, keyPair.private)
val decryptedData = cipher.doFinal(encryptedData)
val decryptedText = String(decryptedData)
```

Best Practices for Data Encryption

Use Strong Encryption Algorithms: Always use strong, industry-standard encryption algorithms. AES with a 256-bit key is recommended for symmetric encryption, while RSA is suitable for asymmetric encryption.

Key Management: Utilize the Android Keystore for managing cryptographic keys securely. Avoid hardcoding keys or storing them in plaintext within your application.

User Authentication: Consider requiring user authentication for accessing sensitive data or performing encryption/decryption operations. This adds an extra layer of security.

Secure Data Storage: Use the Jetpack Security library for securely storing sensitive data, particularly when using SharedPreferences. This helps to mitigate risks associated with plaintext storage.

Regularly Update Dependencies: Ensure you are using the latest versions of libraries, as updates may include security patches and improvements.

Incorporating encryption into your Android applications is essential for protecting sensitive user data. By leveraging the Jetpack Security library in conjunction with the Android Keystore system, developers can implement robust encryption mechanisms with relative ease. The combination of these tools not only simplifies the encryption process but also enhances the security of cryptographic keys and sensitive data storage. By following best practices for data encryption, you can build secure applications that safeguard user privacy and data integrity, thereby building trust and confidence in your app.

9.2 Implementing Biometric Authentication

Biometric authentication is becoming increasingly essential in modern mobile applications, offering users a convenient and secure way to access their accounts and sensitive data. With Android's built-in biometric features, developers can implement fingerprint, facial recognition, or iris scanning functionalities. This chapter explores how to integrate biometric authentication into your Android applications, enhancing security and user experience.

Understanding Biometric Authentication

Biometric authentication uses unique biological characteristics, such as fingerprints or facial features, to verify a user's identity. Compared to traditional authentication methods like passwords or PINs, biometric methods provide several advantages:

- **Enhanced Security**: Biometric data is difficult to replicate, making unauthorized access more challenging.
- **Convenience**: Users can quickly authenticate without remembering complex passwords or patterns.
- **Reduced Friction**: Biometric methods streamline the login process, improving overall user experience.

Android provides a standardized way to implement biometric authentication through the BiometricPrompt API, which supports fingerprint, face, and iris recognition, depending on the device capabilities.

Setting Up Biometric Authentication

To use biometric authentication in your Android application, follow these steps:

Add the Required Dependencies: Ensure that you have the necessary dependencies in your build.gradle file. The BiometricPrompt API is included in the AndroidX Biometric library:

```
dependencies {
    implementation "androidx.biometric:biometric:1.1.0"
}
```

Check Biometric Availability: Before implementing the authentication flow, check whether biometric authentication is available on the device. This involves verifying the hardware capability and whether the user has enrolled any biometric data.

```
val biometricManager = BiometricManager.from(context)
when (biometricManager.canAuthenticate()) {
    BiometricManager.Authenticators.BIOMETRIC_SUCCESS -> {
        // Biometric authentication is available and the user has enrolled biometrics
    }
    BiometricManager.Authenticators.BIOMETRIC_ERROR_NO_HARDWARE -> {
        // Device does not have biometric hardware
    }
    BiometricManager.Authenticators.BIOMETRIC_ERROR_NONE_ENROLLED -> {
        // No biometric credentials enrolled
    }
}
```

Create a BiometricPrompt Instance: Use the BiometricPrompt class to initiate the authentication process. This class requires a callback to handle the results of the authentication attempt.

```
val executor = ContextCompat.getMainExecutor(context)
val biometricPrompt = BiometricPrompt(activity, executor, object :
BiometricPrompt.AuthenticationCallback() {
```

```kotlin
    override fun onAuthenticationError(errorCode: Int, errString: CharSequence) {
        super.onAuthenticationError(errorCode, errString)
        // Handle authentication error
        Log.e("BiometricPrompt", "Authentication error: $errString")
    }

    override fun onAuthenticationSucceeded(result:
BiometricPrompt.AuthenticationResult) {
        super.onAuthenticationSucceeded(result)
        // Handle successful authentication
        Log.d("BiometricPrompt", "Authentication succeeded")
    }

    override fun onAuthenticationFailed() {
        super.onAuthenticationFailed()
        // Handle authentication failure
        Log.e("BiometricPrompt", "Authentication failed")
    }
})
```

Build the Authentication Dialog: Create a BiometricPrompt.PromptInfo instance to define the authentication prompt, including title, subtitle, and confirmation message.

```kotlin
val promptInfo = BiometricPrompt.PromptInfo.Builder()
    .setTitle("Biometric Login")
    .setSubtitle("Log in using your biometric credential")
    .setNegativeButtonText("Use account password")
    .build()
```

Authenticate the User: Finally, trigger the authentication process using the authenticate() method of the BiometricPrompt instance.

```kotlin
biometricPrompt.authenticate(promptInfo)
```

Handling Authentication Results

When implementing biometric authentication, it's essential to handle various outcomes appropriately:

Authentication Success: Upon successful authentication, you should grant the user access to the sensitive data or functionality.

Authentication Failure: If the authentication fails, you can prompt the user to try again or offer alternative methods, such as entering a password.

Authentication Errors: Different types of errors can occur, such as hardware not being available or the user not having enrolled any biometrics. Handle these gracefully, informing the user of the situation.

Best Practices for Biometric Authentication

Fallback Options: Always provide a fallback authentication method, such as a password or PIN, to ensure users can access their accounts even if biometric authentication fails.

User Experience: Use biometric authentication judiciously to enhance user experience without compromising security. For instance, allow users to enable or disable biometric login in the app settings.

Security: Be aware that biometric data cannot be modified or reset like passwords. Hence, ensure that sensitive operations are safeguarded by biometric authentication, and consider implementing a timeout for sensitive actions after several failed attempts.

Privacy Considerations: Clearly inform users about how their biometric data will be used and stored. Ensure compliance with data protection regulations such as GDPR, which mandates user consent for processing personal data.

Example Implementation

Here's a complete example of how to implement biometric authentication in an Android application:

```
class MainActivity : AppCompatActivity() {

    override fun onCreate(savedInstanceState: Bundle?) {
        super.onCreate(savedInstanceState)
        setContentView(R.layout.activity_main)

        // Check biometric availability
        checkBiometricAvailability()
```

```kotlin
        // Button to trigger authentication
        val loginButton: Button = findViewById(R.id.login_button)
        loginButton.setOnClickListener { authenticateUser() }
    }

    private fun checkBiometricAvailability() {
        val biometricManager = BiometricManager.from(this)
        when (biometricManager.canAuthenticate()) {
            BiometricManager.Authenticators.BIOMETRIC_SUCCESS -> {
                // Ready for authentication
            }
            BiometricManager.Authenticators.BIOMETRIC_ERROR_NO_HARDWARE -> {
                // No biometric hardware
            }
            BiometricManager.Authenticators.BIOMETRIC_ERROR_NONE_ENROLLED ->
{
                // No biometrics enrolled
            }
        }
    }

    private fun authenticateUser() {
        val executor = ContextCompat.getMainExecutor(this)
        val biometricPrompt = BiometricPrompt(this, executor, object :
BiometricPrompt.AuthenticationCallback() {
            override fun onAuthenticationError(errorCode: Int, errString: CharSequence) {
                super.onAuthenticationError(errorCode, errString)
                Toast.makeText(applicationContext, "Authentication error: $errString",
Toast.LENGTH_SHORT).show()
            }

            override fun onAuthenticationSucceeded(result:
BiometricPrompt.AuthenticationResult) {
                super.onAuthenticationSucceeded(result)
                Toast.makeText(applicationContext, "Authentication succeeded",
Toast.LENGTH_SHORT).show()
                // Proceed to the next activity or show protected content
            }
```

```
        override fun onAuthenticationFailed() {
            super.onAuthenticationFailed()
            Toast.makeText(applicationContext, "Authentication failed",
Toast.LENGTH_SHORT).show()
        }
    })

    val promptInfo = BiometricPrompt.PromptInfo.Builder()
        .setTitle("Biometric Login")
        .setSubtitle("Log in using your biometric credential")
        .setNegativeButtonText("Use account password")
        .build()

    biometricPrompt.authenticate(promptInfo)
    }
}
```

Implementing biometric authentication in your Android application can significantly enhance security and provide a better user experience. By leveraging the BiometricPrompt API and following best practices, developers can create robust authentication flows that are both secure and user-friendly. As biometric technology continues to evolve, integrating these features into applications will not only meet user expectations for security but also promote trust in your app's handling of sensitive data.

9.3 Securing Network Communication and Handling Sensitive Data

In the era of mobile applications, securing network communication and handling sensitive data has never been more critical. With an increasing amount of personal and sensitive information being exchanged over the internet, Android developers must implement robust security measures to protect user data during transmission and storage. This chapter will explore the best practices for securing network communication and handling sensitive data within Android applications.

Understanding the Risks

Network communication in mobile applications involves transmitting data over potentially insecure channels, making it vulnerable to interception, eavesdropping, and tampering. Common risks include:

- **Man-in-the-Middle (MitM) Attacks**: Attackers can intercept communication between the client and server to gain unauthorized access to sensitive data.
- **Data Leakage**: Sensitive information, if not properly encrypted, can be exposed during transmission or stored insecurely on the device.
- **Replay Attacks**: Attackers can capture and resend requests to manipulate application behavior.

To mitigate these risks, developers must adopt a multi-faceted approach that combines encryption, secure communication protocols, and best practices for handling sensitive data.

Securing Network Communication

Use HTTPS: The foundation of secure network communication is HTTPS (HTTP over SSL/TLS). HTTPS encrypts data transmitted between the client and server, protecting it from eavesdropping and tampering.

To implement HTTPS in your Android application, ensure that your server supports SSL/TLS. Then, make network requests using libraries that support HTTPS, such as Retrofit or OkHttp.

```
val retrofit = Retrofit.Builder()
    .baseUrl("https://api.example.com/")
    .addConverterFactory(GsonConverterFactory.create())
    .build()
```

Certificate Pinning: To prevent MitM attacks, consider implementing certificate pinning. This process involves embedding the server's SSL certificate or public key in the application. When a connection is made, the app verifies the server's certificate against the pinned certificate.

In OkHttp, you can configure certificate pinning as follows:

```
val certificatePinner = CertificatePinner.Builder()
    .add("api.example.com",
"sha256/AAAAAAAAAAAAAAAAAAAAAAAAAAAAAAAAAAAAAAAAAAA=")
```

```
  .build()

val client = OkHttpClient.Builder()
  .certificatePinner(certificatePinner)
  .build()
```

Implementing Secure Communication Protocols: Use secure communication protocols such as OAuth2 for authentication and authorization. This ensures that sensitive data, such as tokens and user credentials, are transmitted securely.

Use Secure WebSockets: If your application requires real-time communication, consider using secure WebSockets (WSS). WebSockets allow for full-duplex communication channels over a single TCP connection and should always be implemented over a secure connection.

```
val request = Request.Builder().url("wss://api.example.com/socket").build()
val client = OkHttpClient()

val webSocket = client.newWebSocket(request, object : WebSocketListener() {
    override fun onOpen(webSocket: WebSocket, response: Response) {
        // Connection established
    }
})
```

Data Encryption: For particularly sensitive data, consider encrypting the data before transmission. Use strong encryption algorithms like AES or RSA to protect the data at rest and in transit.

Handling Sensitive Data

Use Android Keystore: When handling sensitive data such as API keys, tokens, and user credentials, utilize the Android Keystore system. This allows you to securely store cryptographic keys without exposing them to the app's code.

Generate and store keys in the Keystore:

```
val keyGenParameterSpec = KeyGenParameterSpec.Builder(
    "my_key_alias",
    KeyProperties.PURPOSE_ENCRYPT or KeyProperties.PURPOSE_DECRYPT
)
```

```
.setBlockModes(KeyProperties.BLOCK_MODE_GCM)
.setEncryptionPaddings(KeyProperties.ENCRYPTION_PADDING_NONE)
.build()

val keyGenerator = KeyGenerator.getInstance(KeyProperties.KEY_ALGORITHM_AES,
"AndroidKeyStore")
keyGenerator.init(keyGenParameterSpec)
val secretKey = keyGenerator.generateKey()
```

Data Protection with Encrypted SharedPreferences: Store sensitive information securely using EncryptedSharedPreferences. This ensures that any data written to SharedPreferences is encrypted automatically.

```
val masterKeyAlias = MasterKey.Builder(context)
  .setKeyScheme(MasterKey.KeyScheme.AES256_GCM)
  .build()

val sharedPreferences = EncryptedSharedPreferences.create(
  context,
  "secure_prefs",
  masterKeyAlias,
  EncryptedSharedPreferences.PrefKeyEncryptionScheme.AES256_SIV,
  EncryptedSharedPreferences.PrefValueEncryptionScheme.AES256_GCM
)

// Store sensitive data
with(sharedPreferences.edit()) {
  putString("api_token", "secure_token")
  apply()
}
```

Secure API Keys and Secrets: Avoid hardcoding sensitive information, such as API keys or secrets, in your code. Instead, consider using build configuration files or remote configuration services.

Regularly Review Permissions: Ensure that your application requests only the permissions necessary for its functionality. Excessive permissions can lead to security vulnerabilities.

User Education: Educate users about the importance of security, such as not sharing passwords or sensitive information and recognizing phishing attempts.

Best Practices for Securing Network Communication

Use Strong Encryption Protocols: Always opt for strong encryption standards such as TLS 1.2 or higher for network communication.

Validate SSL Certificates: Always validate the SSL certificates returned from the server to prevent certificate spoofing.

Implement Logging and Monitoring: Regularly log and monitor network communications for suspicious activity or unauthorized access attempts.

Update Dependencies Regularly: Keep your dependencies and libraries up to date to ensure that any security vulnerabilities are patched.

Conduct Security Testing: Regularly perform security testing, including penetration testing, to identify and address potential vulnerabilities.

Securing network communication and handling sensitive data is essential for protecting user privacy and maintaining trust in your Android applications. By implementing robust security measures, including HTTPS, certificate pinning, and utilizing the Android Keystore, developers can significantly reduce the risks associated with data transmission and storage. Moreover, adhering to best practices and continuously monitoring and updating security protocols ensures that applications remain secure in an evolving threat landscape. By prioritizing security in your application development process, you create a safer environment for your users, enhancing their overall experience.

Chapter 10: Location and Map-Based Features with Google Maps API

In this chapter, we will explore how to integrate location-based features into your Android applications using the Google Maps API. You will learn how to set up and customize Google Maps within your app, including adding markers, polylines, and polygons to visualize data spatially. We'll delve into the various functionalities of the Maps SDK, such as handling user interactions, implementing camera movements, and responding to map events. Additionally, we will cover how to utilize Android's Location Services to provide real-time location tracking, geofencing, and managing location permissions effectively. By leveraging these tools, you can create applications that offer dynamic, context-aware experiences, such as navigation and location-based recommendations. Furthermore, we will discuss best practices for optimizing map performance and user experience, including considerations for offline maps and data caching. By the end of this chapter, you will be equipped with the skills to build rich, interactive map features that enhance user engagement and provide valuable location-based services in your Android applications.

10.1 Integrating Google Maps and Customizing Map Views

Integrating Google Maps into your Android application can greatly enhance user experience by providing dynamic location-based services. Whether your app requires basic mapping functionalities, location tracking, or complex geospatial interactions, the Google Maps API offers extensive features that can be tailored to meet your needs. In this section, we will explore how to integrate Google Maps into your Android app, customize map views, and implement various functionalities.

Getting Started with Google Maps API

To use Google Maps in your Android application, you first need to set up a project on Google Cloud Console and obtain an API key. Here's a step-by-step guide to get started:

Create a Google Cloud Project:

- Go to the Google Cloud Console.
- Click on "Select a project" and then "New Project."
- Name your project and click "Create."

Enable the Maps SDK for Android:

In your project dashboard, navigate to the "Library" section.

Search for "Maps SDK for Android" and enable it.

Obtain an API Key:

- Go to the "Credentials" section in the left sidebar.
- Click "Create credentials" and select "API key."
- Restrict your API key to prevent unauthorized use (e.g., by package name).

Add Dependencies:

Open your build.gradle file (Module: app) and add the Google Play Services dependency:

```
dependencies {
    implementation 'com.google.android.gms:play-services-maps:18.0.2'
}
```

Add Permissions:

Ensure you have the necessary permissions in your AndroidManifest.xml file:

```
<uses-permission android:name="android.permission.INTERNET"/>
<uses-permission android:name="android.permission.ACCESS_FINE_LOCATION"/>
<uses-permission
android:name="android.permission.ACCESS_COARSE_LOCATION"/>
```

Include the API Key:

Also in your AndroidManifest.xml, add the metadata tag within the <application> tag:

```
<meta-data
    android:name="com.google.android.geo.API_KEY"
    android:value="YOUR_API_KEY_HERE"/>
```

Setting Up a Basic Map

Once you have the API key and necessary configurations set up, you can create a simple map activity:

Create a Layout for the Map:

In your activity_maps.xml, add a MapFragment or SupportMapFragment:

```
<fragment
    xmlns:android="http://schemas.android.com/apk/res/android"
    android:id="@+id/map"
    android:name="com.google.android.gms.maps.SupportMapFragment"
    android:layout_width="match_parent"
    android:layout_height="match_parent"/>
```

Implement the Map in Your Activity:

In your MapsActivity.java or MapsActivity.kt, initialize the map in the onCreate method:

```
class MapsActivity : AppCompatActivity(), OnMapReadyCallback {

    private lateinit var mMap: GoogleMap

    override fun onCreate(savedInstanceState: Bundle?) {
        super.onCreate(savedInstanceState)
        setContentView(R.layout.activity_maps)

        // Obtain the SupportMapFragment and get notified when the map is ready to be used.
        val mapFragment = supportFragmentManager
            .findFragmentById(R.id.map) as SupportMapFragment
        mapFragment.getMapAsync(this)
    }

    override fun onMapReady(googleMap: GoogleMap) {
        mMap = googleMap

        // Add a marker in a specific location (e.g., Sydney) and move the camera
        val sydney = LatLng(-34.0, 151.0)
        mMap.addMarker(MarkerOptions().position(sydney).title("Marker in Sydney"))
        mMap.moveCamera(CameraUpdateFactory.newLatLng(sydney))
```

```
    }
}
```

Customizing Map Views

Google Maps offers a wide range of customization options to tailor the map to your application's needs:

Changing Map Types:

You can set different map types to provide varying views (e.g., normal, satellite, terrain, hybrid).

mMap.mapType = GoogleMap.MAP_TYPE_SATELLITE

Adding Markers:

Markers can be customized by changing their icons, titles, and snippets.

val customIcon = BitmapDescriptorFactory.fromResource(R.drawable.custom_marker)
mMap.addMarker(MarkerOptions()
  .position(sydney)
  .title("Custom Marker")
  .icon(customIcon))

Drawing Polylines and Polygons:

You can visually represent routes and areas on the map using polylines and polygons.

val polylineOptions = PolylineOptions()
  .add(LatLng(-34.0, 151.0))
  .add(LatLng(-34.5, 151.5))
  .width(5f)
  .color(Color.BLUE)
mMap.addPolyline(polylineOptions)

val polygonOptions = PolygonOptions()
  .add(LatLng(-34.0, 151.0), LatLng(-34.5, 151.0), LatLng(-34.5, 151.5))
  .strokeColor(Color.RED)
  .fillColor(Color.argb(70, 150, 0, 0))

mMap.addPolygon(polygonOptions)

Setting Up Location Tracking:

To enhance user experience, you can implement user location tracking. This requires location permissions and enabling the location layer.

```
if (ActivityCompat.checkSelfPermission(this,
Manifest.permission.ACCESS_FINE_LOCATION) !=
PackageManager.PERMISSION_GRANTED
    && ActivityCompat.checkSelfPermission(this,
Manifest.permission.ACCESS_COARSE_LOCATION) !=
PackageManager.PERMISSION_GRANTED) {
    ActivityCompat.requestPermissions(this,
arrayOf(Manifest.permission.ACCESS_FINE_LOCATION),
LOCATION_PERMISSION_REQUEST_CODE)
    return
}
mMap.isMyLocationEnabled = true
```

Customizing Map UI:

You can hide or show various UI components of the map, such as the compass, my-location button, and zoom controls.

```
mMap.uiSettings.isZoomControlsEnabled = true
mMap.uiSettings.isMyLocationButtonEnabled = true
```

Advanced Customizations

Using Map Style JSON:

Google Maps allows you to customize the appearance of your map using a Map Style JSON. This can change colors, visibility of features, and more.

```
val success = mMap.setMapStyle(MapStyleOptions.loadRawResourceStyle(this,
R.raw.map_style))
if (!success) {
    Log.e(TAG, "Style parsing failed.")
}
```

Implementing Click Listeners:

Adding listeners for marker clicks, map clicks, and other events allows you to create interactive experiences.

```
mMap.setOnMarkerClickListener { marker ->
    Toast.makeText(this, "Clicked: ${marker.title}", Toast.LENGTH_SHORT).show()
    true
}
```

Clustering Markers:

If you have numerous markers to display, consider using the Marker Clustering utility to improve performance and usability.

```
val clusterManager = ClusterManager<MyClusterItem>(this, mMap)
mMap.setOnCameraIdleListener(clusterManager)
mMap.setOnMarkerClickListener(clusterManager)
```

Integrating Google Maps into your Android application opens up a world of possibilities for location-based services and user interactions. By following the steps outlined in this section, you can easily set up Google Maps, customize map views, and implement advanced functionalities to enhance user experience. As you develop your application, always consider usability, performance, and security to ensure a seamless and efficient mapping experience. With Google Maps, you can create rich, interactive, and location-aware applications that engage users and provide valuable insights into their surroundings.

10.2 Using Location Services and Permissions for Real-Time Updates

Incorporating real-time location services into your Android application allows you to provide users with timely and relevant information based on their geographical position. Whether it's for navigation, location-based services, or personalized user experiences, leveraging location services is essential. In this section, we will explore how to implement location services in your app, manage user permissions, and ensure a smooth experience with real-time updates.

Understanding Android Location Services

Android offers various APIs to retrieve location data, primarily through the Fused Location Provider. This API combines signals from GPS, Wi-Fi, and cell networks to provide the most accurate location data available while optimizing for power consumption.

Key features of the Fused Location Provider include:

- **High Accuracy**: Combines multiple sources for accurate location tracking.
- **Battery Efficiency**: Uses less battery compared to GPS alone by prioritizing Wi-Fi and cellular data when available.
- **Flexible Location Requests**: Supports different levels of accuracy based on user needs, such as high accuracy for navigation and low accuracy for geofencing.

Setting Up Location Services

Add Necessary Permissions:

To access the user's location, you need to declare the appropriate permissions in your AndroidManifest.xml file. Starting with Android 6.0 (API level 23), location permissions must be requested at runtime.

```
<uses-permission android:name="android.permission.ACCESS_FINE_LOCATION"/>
<uses-permission
android:name="android.permission.ACCESS_COARSE_LOCATION"/>
```

Requesting Location Permissions:

Check if permissions are granted before attempting to access the user's location. If not, request them at runtime.

```
private fun requestLocationPermissions() {
   if (ActivityCompat.checkSelfPermission(this,
Manifest.permission.ACCESS_FINE_LOCATION) !=
PackageManager.PERMISSION_GRANTED) {
      ActivityCompat.requestPermissions(this,
arrayOf(Manifest.permission.ACCESS_FINE_LOCATION),
LOCATION_PERMISSION_REQUEST_CODE)
   } else {
```

```kotlin
      // Permissions already granted
      startLocationUpdates()
   }
}
```

Implementing Location Callback:

Set up a LocationCallback to receive location updates. The FusedLocationProviderClient is used to request location updates and handle the results.

```kotlin
private lateinit var fusedLocationClient: FusedLocationProviderClient
private lateinit var locationCallback: LocationCallback

private fun startLocationUpdates() {
   fusedLocationClient = LocationServices.getFusedLocationProviderClient(this)

   locationCallback = object : LocationCallback() {
      override fun onLocationResult(locationResult: LocationResult?) {
         locationResult ?: return
         for (location in locationResult.locations) {
            // Handle location updates here
            updateUIWithLocation(location)
         }
      }
   }

   val locationRequest = LocationRequest.create().apply {
      interval = 10000 // 10 seconds
      fastestInterval = 5000 // 5 seconds
      priority = LocationRequest.PRIORITY_HIGH_ACCURACY
   }

   // Start location updates
   fusedLocationClient.requestLocationUpdates(locationRequest, locationCallback,
Looper.getMainLooper())
}
```

Handling Location Updates

Updating UI with Location Data:

Use the received location data to update your UI or perform actions based on the user's location. For instance, you can show the user's current location on a map, provide directions, or update nearby location suggestions.

```
private fun updateUIWithLocation(location: Location) {
    val latLng = LatLng(location.latitude, location.longitude)
    mMap.moveCamera(CameraUpdateFactory.newLatLng(latLng))
    // Additional UI updates can go here
}
```

Stopping Location Updates:

To conserve battery, it's essential to stop location updates when they are no longer needed. You can do this in the onPause() method of your activity.

```
override fun onPause() {
    super.onPause()
    fusedLocationClient.removeLocationUpdates(locationCallback)
}
```

Implementing Background Location Updates

For applications requiring location updates while in the background (e.g., fitness trackers, navigation apps), ensure you handle permissions and optimizations correctly:

Background Location Permissions:

Starting from Android 10 (API level 29), you must request the ACCESS_BACKGROUND_LOCATION permission if your app needs to access location while in the background.

```
<uses-permission
android:name="android.permission.ACCESS_BACKGROUND_LOCATION"/>
```

Requesting Background Location:

Similar to foreground permissions, you must request background permissions at runtime.

```
private fun requestBackgroundLocationPermission() {
```

```
    if (ActivityCompat.checkSelfPermission(this,
Manifest.permission.ACCESS_BACKGROUND_LOCATION) !=
PackageManager.PERMISSION_GRANTED) {
        ActivityCompat.requestPermissions(this,
arrayOf(Manifest.permission.ACCESS_BACKGROUND_LOCATION),
BACKGROUND_LOCATION_PERMISSION_REQUEST_CODE)
    } else {
        // Background permission granted
        startLocationUpdates()
    }
}
```

Using Foreground Services:

For continuous background location updates, implement a foreground service to keep your app active while tracking locations. This approach also shows a persistent notification to inform users about the ongoing location tracking.

```
private fun startForegroundService() {
    val serviceIntent = Intent(this, LocationUpdatesService::class.java)
    ContextCompat.startForegroundService(this, serviceIntent)
}
```

Best Practices for Location Services

Optimize for Battery Life:

Use appropriate location request intervals and accuracy settings to minimize battery consumption. Adjust the frequency of location updates based on user activity (e.g., lower frequency while stationary).

Respect User Privacy:

Always inform users why your app requires location access and how it will use their data. Implement options for users to enable or disable location tracking.

Handle Permissions Gracefully:

Be prepared for users to deny location permissions. Implement fallback mechanisms or guide users to settings where they can enable permissions.

Monitor Location Accuracy:

Consider allowing users to select the level of accuracy they prefer, especially for applications that do not require high accuracy (e.g., geofencing).

Test on Different Devices:

Location services may behave differently across devices and Android versions. Test your implementation on multiple devices to ensure a consistent experience.

Integrating real-time location services into your Android application enhances user engagement by providing relevant and personalized experiences. By leveraging the Fused Location Provider, handling user permissions effectively, and optimizing for battery life, you can implement robust location-based features. Always prioritize user privacy and experience, ensuring that location tracking is transparent and meaningful. With the right approach, your application can provide valuable insights based on the user's real-time location, creating a dynamic and interactive experience.

10.3 Advanced Map Features: Geofencing, Polylines, and Clustering

Incorporating advanced features into your Android application using Google Maps can significantly enhance its functionality and user engagement. This section focuses on three powerful capabilities: geofencing, polylines for visualizing paths or routes, and marker clustering for managing large datasets on the map. Each feature serves a unique purpose and can be integrated into various types of applications, from logistics and transportation to social networking and local discovery.

1. Geofencing

Geofencing enables your application to create virtual boundaries around specific geographic areas. When users enter or exit these boundaries, your app can trigger predefined actions, such as sending notifications, updating the UI, or logging events. This is particularly useful for location-based services, marketing, or tracking user behavior.

Setting Up Geofencing

Add Dependencies: To use geofencing, include the following dependencies in your build.gradle file:

```
implementation 'com.google.android.gms:play-services-location:19.0.1'
```

Define Geofence Data: You can define geofences by specifying their latitude, longitude, radius, and transition types (e.g., entering or exiting).

```
val geofence = Geofence.Builder()
  .setRequestId("Geofence_ID")
  .setCircularRegion(
    latitude,
    longitude,
    radius // in meters
  )
  .setExpirationDuration(Geofence.NEVER_EXPIRE)
  .setTransitionTypes(Geofence.GEOFENCE_TRANSITION_ENTER or
Geofence.GEOFENCE_TRANSITION_EXIT)
  .build()
```

Create a Geofencing Request: Once you have defined the geofence, create a request to add it to the Geofencing API.

```
val geofencingRequest = GeofencingRequest.Builder()
  .setInitialTrigger(GeofencingRequest.INITIAL_TRIGGER_ENTER)
  .addGeofence(geofence)
  .build()
```

Add Geofences: Use the GeofencingClient to add the geofences and handle results with a callback.

```
val geofencingClient = LocationServices.getGeofencingClient(this)

geofencingClient.addGeofences(geofencingRequest, geofencePendingIntent)
  .addOnSuccessListener {
    // Geofences added
  }
  .addOnFailureListener {
    // Handle failure
  }
```

Handle Geofence Transitions: Create a BroadcastReceiver to respond to geofence transitions, allowing you to trigger notifications or actions when the user enters or exits a geofenced area.

```
class GeofenceBroadcastReceiver : BroadcastReceiver() {
    override fun onReceive(context: Context, intent: Intent) {
        // Handle geofence transition
    }
}
```

Register the Receiver: Ensure that your BroadcastReceiver is registered in the AndroidManifest.xml.

```
<receiver android:name=".GeofenceBroadcastReceiver"/>
```

2. Polylines

Polylines are used to visually represent paths or routes on a map. They can be particularly useful for applications that require tracking routes, such as navigation apps or fitness trackers.

Drawing Polylines on the Map

Creating a Polyline: Use the PolylineOptions class to define the polyline's appearance (color, width) and coordinates.

```
val polylineOptions = PolylineOptions()
    .add(LatLng(startLat, startLng))
    .add(LatLng(intermediateLat1, intermediateLng1))
    .add(LatLng(intermediateLat2, intermediateLng2))
    .add(LatLng(endLat, endLng))
    .width(10f)
    .color(Color.BLUE)
```

Adding the Polyline to the Map: Once you have your PolylineOptions, add the polyline to the map.

```
val polyline = mMap.addPolyline(polylineOptions)
```

Dynamic Updates: If your application requires real-time updates (e.g., tracking user movements), you can update the polyline dynamically by modifying its points.

```
val points = mutableListOf<LatLng>()
// Update points based on user location
polyline.points = points
```

3. Marker Clustering

Marker clustering is essential for managing and displaying large datasets on the map without cluttering the interface. Clustering groups nearby markers into a single marker (a cluster), which can be expanded when zoomed in.

Setting Up Marker Clustering

Add Dependencies: Include the marker clustering dependency in your build.gradle.

```
implementation 'com.google.maps.android:android-maps-utils:2.2.1'
```

Create Cluster Manager: Initialize a ClusterManager to handle clustering and manage the markers.

```
val clusterManager = ClusterManager<MyClusterItem>(this, mMap)
mMap.setOnCameraIdleListener(clusterManager)
mMap.setOnMarkerClickListener(clusterManager)
```

Defining Cluster Item: Implement a class that extends ClusterItem to define your markers.

```
class MyClusterItem(
    private val position: LatLng,
    private val title: String,
    private val snippet: String
) : ClusterItem {
    override fun getPosition() = position
    override fun getTitle() = title
    override fun getSnippet() = snippet
}
```

Adding Items to the Cluster: Add your cluster items to the ClusterManager and trigger the clustering algorithm.

```
fun addItemsToCluster() {
    val item1 = MyClusterItem(LatLng(34.0, -118.0), "Title 1", "Snippet 1")
    val item2 = MyClusterItem(LatLng(34.1, -118.1), "Title 2", "Snippet 2")
    clusterManager.addItem(item1)
    clusterManager.addItem(item2)
}
```

Handling Cluster Clicks: You can define behavior for when a cluster or individual marker is clicked.

```
clusterManager.setOnClusterClickListener { cluster ->
    // Handle cluster click
    true
}
```

```
clusterManager.setOnClusterItemClickListener { item ->
    // Handle individual marker click
    true
}
```

Implementing advanced map features like geofencing, polylines, and clustering significantly enhances the functionality of your Android application. Geofencing allows you to create interactive experiences based on users' physical locations, while polylines help visualize routes effectively. Marker clustering addresses the challenge of displaying large datasets on maps, ensuring a clean and user-friendly interface. By leveraging these features, you can create engaging and practical location-based applications that enhance user experience and provide valuable services. Whether you're building a navigation tool, a fitness tracker, or a location-based service, these advanced map features can be crucial in delivering a comprehensive user experience.

Chapter 11: Integrating Machine Learning with ML Kit and TensorFlow Lite

In this chapter, we will explore how to incorporate machine learning capabilities into your Android applications using ML Kit and TensorFlow Lite. You will begin by learning about ML Kit, Google's mobile SDK that provides easy-to-use APIs for implementing common machine learning functionalities such as image labeling, text recognition, face detection, and barcode scanning. We'll cover how to set up ML Kit in your project and integrate its pre-built models to enhance your applications without requiring deep knowledge of machine learning. Next, we will delve into TensorFlow Lite, the lightweight version of TensorFlow designed for mobile and edge devices. You'll learn how to convert and optimize custom machine learning models for use on Android, enabling you to implement more complex functionalities tailored to your specific needs. We will also discuss best practices for optimizing model performance and ensuring efficient use of device resources. By the end of this chapter, you will have the knowledge and tools necessary to build smart, responsive applications that leverage the power of machine learning, providing users with cutting-edge features that enhance their experience and interaction with your app.

11.1 Setting Up and Implementing ML Kit APIs

Machine Learning (ML) is revolutionizing the way mobile applications operate, providing advanced capabilities that can improve user experiences, automate tasks, and deliver valuable insights. Google's ML Kit offers a suite of powerful APIs designed to simplify the implementation of machine learning models for Android applications. In this section, we will discuss how to set up ML Kit in your project, explore its available APIs, and provide practical examples of how to implement these APIs effectively.

1. Setting Up ML Kit in Your Android Project

To begin using ML Kit, you must set up your Android project with the required dependencies and configurations.

Step 1: Add Dependencies

Open your build.gradle (Module: app) file and add the necessary ML Kit dependencies. Depending on the APIs you want to use, include the following:

```
dependencies {
    implementation 'com.google.firebase:firebase-ml-vision:24.0.3' // For ML Kit Vision
APIs
    implementation 'com.google.firebase:firebase-ml-natural-language:22.0.1' // For
Natural Language APIs
    implementation 'com.google.firebase:firebase-ml-model-interpreter:22.0.1' // For
Custom Models
}
```

Sync your project to download the dependencies.

Step 2: Enable Firebase in Your Project

ML Kit is built on top of Firebase, so you need to integrate Firebase into your Android project:

Go to the Firebase Console.

Create a new project or select an existing one.

Add an Android app to your Firebase project and follow the instructions to download the google-services.json file.

Place the google-services.json file in your app's app/ directory.

Add the Firebase plugin to your build.gradle (Project) file:

```
buildscript {
    dependencies {
        // Add this line
        classpath 'com.google.gms:google-services:4.3.14'
    }
}
```

At the bottom of your build.gradle (Module: app) file, apply the Google services plugin:

```
apply plugin: 'com.google.gms.google-services'
```

Step 3: Configure Permissions

Depending on the ML Kit APIs you plan to use (e.g., Camera API for image analysis), ensure that your AndroidManifest.xml includes the required permissions:

<uses-permission android:name="android.permission.CAMERA" />
<uses-permission android:name="android.permission.INTERNET" />

2. Exploring ML Kit APIs

ML Kit provides several ready-to-use APIs that you can integrate into your app, including:

- **Vision APIs**: For image labeling, text recognition, face detection, barcode scanning, and more.
- **Natural Language APIs**: For language identification, smart reply, entity extraction, and sentiment analysis.
- **Custom Model APIs**: For deploying and using your own TensorFlow Lite models.
- **Example**: Implementing Image Labeling API

Let's explore a simple example of how to use the ML Kit Vision API for image labeling.

Step 1: Set Up the Image Labeling API

Create a method to perform image labeling. You can either use an image from the gallery or capture one using the camera.

```
private fun labelImage(image: InputImage) {
    val labeler = ImageLabeling.getClient(ImageLabelerOptions.DEFAULT_OPTIONS)

    labeler.process(image)
        .addOnSuccessListener { labels ->
            // Task completed successfully
            for (label in labels) {
                val text = label.text
                val confidence = label.confidence
                Log.d("Labeling", "Label: $text, Confidence: $confidence")
            }
        }
        .addOnFailureListener { e ->
            // Task failed with an exception
```

```
        Log.e("Labeling", "Image labeling failed", e)
    }
}
```

Step 2: Capture or Load an Image

You can load an image from the gallery or capture it using the camera. Here's an example of capturing an image using the camera:

```
private fun captureImage() {
    val cameraIntent = Intent(MediaStore.ACTION_IMAGE_CAPTURE)
    startActivityForResult(cameraIntent, REQUEST_IMAGE_CAPTURE)
}

override fun onActivityResult(requestCode: Int, resultCode: Int, data: Intent?) {
    super.onActivityResult(requestCode, resultCode, data)

    if (requestCode == REQUEST_IMAGE_CAPTURE && resultCode ==
Activity.RESULT_OK) {
        val imageBitmap = data?.extras?.get("data") as Bitmap
        val inputImage = InputImage.fromBitmap(imageBitmap, 0)
        labelImage(inputImage)
    }
}
```

3. Working with Other ML Kit APIs

ML Kit provides a variety of other APIs, and setting them up follows a similar pattern:

Example: Text Recognition

Using the Text Recognition API:

```
private fun recognizeText(image: InputImage) {
    val recognizer =
TextRecognition.getClient(TextRecognizerOptions.DEFAULT_OPTIONS)

    recognizer.process(image)
        .addOnSuccessListener { visionText ->
            Log.d("TextRecognition", "Detected text: ${visionText.text}")
```

```
        }
        .addOnFailureListener { e ->
            Log.e("TextRecognition", "Text recognition failed", e)
        }
}
```

Example: Barcode Scanning

Setting up Barcode Scanning:

```
private fun scanBarcode(image: InputImage) {
    val scanner = BarcodeScanning.getClient()

    scanner.process(image)
        .addOnSuccessListener { barcodes ->
            for (barcode in barcodes) {
                Log.d("BarcodeScanning", "Barcode value: ${barcode.rawValue}")
            }
        }
        .addOnFailureListener { e ->
            Log.e("BarcodeScanning", "Barcode scanning failed", e)
        }
}
```

4. Using Custom Models

If you have specific use cases that are not covered by the existing ML Kit APIs, you can deploy your custom TensorFlow Lite models.

Setting Up a Custom Model

Add TensorFlow Lite dependencies in your build.gradle:

```
implementation 'org.tensorflow:tensorflow-lite:2.9.0'
implementation 'org.tensorflow:tensorflow-lite-gpu:2.9.0' // Optional for GPU
```

Load and Run the Model:

```
private fun runCustomModel() {
    val model = Interpreter(loadModelFile("model.tflite"))
```

```
    // Prepare input and output tensors
    val input = arrayOf( /* Your input data */ )
    val output = arrayOf( /* Your output data */ )

    model.run(input, output)
}

private fun loadModelFile(modelPath: String): MappedByteBuffer {
    val fileDescriptor = assets.openFd(modelPath)
    val inputStream = FileInputStream(fileDescriptor.fileDescriptor)
    val fileChannel = inputStream.channel
    val startOffset = fileDescriptor.startOffset
    val declaredLength = fileDescriptor.declaredLength
    return fileChannel.map(FileChannel.MapMode.READ_ONLY, startOffset,
declaredLength)
}
```

Integrating ML Kit into your Android application allows you to leverage powerful machine learning capabilities with minimal effort. Whether you're using built-in APIs for image labeling, text recognition, barcode scanning, or deploying custom models, ML Kit provides a straightforward approach to enhance your app's functionality. As you implement these features, consider experimenting with different ML Kit APIs to find the best fit for your use case and continually iterate based on user feedback and performance analysis. With ML Kit, you can create intelligent applications that provide meaningful insights and improve overall user experiences.

11.2 Integrating Custom Models with TensorFlow Lite

Integrating custom machine learning models into your Android application using TensorFlow Lite (TFLite) allows you to leverage specialized algorithms tailored for your specific use cases, such as image classification, object detection, or natural language processing. This section will guide you through the entire process, from creating a model to integrating it into your Android app.

1. Preparing Your Custom Model

Before integrating a custom model into your Android app, you need to have a trained TensorFlow model ready for conversion into a TFLite format. This typically involves the following steps:

Step 1: Train Your Model

Train a TensorFlow Model: Use TensorFlow to create and train your model. For example, if you are training a convolutional neural network (CNN) for image classification, you might use the following:

```
import tensorflow as tf
from tensorflow.keras import layers, models

# Define the model
model = models.Sequential([
    layers.Conv2D(32, (3, 3), activation='relu', input_shape=(img_height, img_width, 3)),
    layers.MaxPooling2D(pool_size=(2, 2)),
    layers.Flatten(),
    layers.Dense(64, activation='relu'),
    layers.Dense(num_classes, activation='softmax')
])

# Compile the model
model.compile(optimizer='adam', loss='sparse_categorical_crossentropy',
metrics=['accuracy'])

# Train the model
model.fit(train_data, train_labels, epochs=10)
```

Save the Model: After training your model, save it in TensorFlow's SavedModel format or as a Keras model.

```
model.save('my_model')
```

Step 2: Convert the Model to TFLite Format

Use the TensorFlow Lite Converter: You can convert your model to TFLite format using the TensorFlow Lite Converter. This process may involve optimization techniques like quantization to reduce the model size and improve performance on mobile devices.

```
converter = tf.lite.TFLiteConverter.from_saved_model('my_model')
tflite_model = converter.convert()
```

```
# Save the converted model
with open('my_model.tflite', 'wb') as f:
    f.write(tflite_model)
```

Optimize the Model (Optional): If needed, apply optimizations like post-training quantization to reduce the model's memory footprint:

```
converter.optimizations = [tf.lite.Optimize.DEFAULT]
```

2. Adding TensorFlow Lite to Your Android Project

To use TensorFlow Lite in your Android app, you must add the necessary dependencies.

Step 1: Add Dependencies

Open your build.gradle (Module: app) file and include the TensorFlow Lite dependencies:

```
dependencies {
    implementation 'org.tensorflow:tensorflow-lite:2.9.0' // Core TFLite library
    implementation 'org.tensorflow:tensorflow-lite-gpu:2.9.0' // Optional: for GPU support
    implementation 'org.tensorflow:tensorflow-lite-support:0.4.0' // Optional: support
library
}
```

Sync your project to download the dependencies.

Step 2: Add the TFLite Model File

Copy the .tflite model file you generated earlier into the assets folder of your Android project. If the assets folder does not exist, create one under src/main/.

3. Loading and Running the Model

With your model added to the project, you can now load and run it within your application.

Step 1: Load the TFLite Model

Load the model in your activity or fragment using the TensorFlow Lite Interpreter:

```
import org.tensorflow.lite.Interpreter
```

```kotlin
import java.nio.MappedByteBuffer
import java.nio.channels.FileChannel
import java.io.FileInputStream

class MyModelActivity : AppCompatActivity() {
    private lateinit var tflite: Interpreter

    override fun onCreate(savedInstanceState: Bundle?) {
        super.onCreate(savedInstanceState)
        setContentView(R.layout.activity_my_model)

        // Load the model
        tflite = Interpreter(loadModelFile("my_model.tflite"))
    }

    private fun loadModelFile(modelPath: String): MappedByteBuffer {
        val fileDescriptor = assets.openFd(modelPath)
        val inputStream = FileInputStream(fileDescriptor.fileDescriptor)
        val fileChannel = inputStream.channel
        val startOffset = fileDescriptor.startOffset
        val declaredLength = fileDescriptor.declaredLength
        return fileChannel.map(FileChannel.MapMode.READ_ONLY, startOffset,
declaredLength)
    }
}
```

Step 2: Prepare Input Data

Prepare the input data for your model. This typically involves resizing, normalizing, and converting the data to the correct format (e.g., float array, byte buffer).

```kotlin
private fun prepareInput(image: Bitmap): Array<FloatArray> {
    val inputSize = 224 // Example input size
    val resizedImage = Bitmap.createScaledBitmap(image, inputSize, inputSize, true)
    val inputArray = Array(1) { FloatArray(inputSize * inputSize * 3) }

    for (y in 0 until inputSize) {
        for (x in 0 until inputSize) {
            val pixel = resizedImage.getPixel(x, y)
            inputArray[0][y * inputSize + x] = Color.red(pixel) / 255.0f
```

```
        inputArray[0][y * inputSize + x + 1] = Color.green(pixel) / 255.0f
        inputArray[0][y * inputSize + x + 2] = Color.blue(pixel) / 255.0f
    }
  }
  return inputArray
}
```

Step 3: Run Inference

Run inference on the input data and obtain the results. Make sure to allocate output buffers as needed.

```
private fun classifyImage(bitmap: Bitmap) {
    val inputArray = prepareInput(bitmap)
    val outputArray = Array(1) { FloatArray(numClasses) } // Adjust numClasses as needed

    // Run the model
    tflite.run(inputArray, outputArray)

    // Process the output
    val result = outputArray[0]
    val predictedClass = result.indices.maxByOrNull { result[it] } ?: -1
    Log.d("ModelPrediction", "Predicted class: $predictedClass with confidence ${result[predictedClass]}")
}
```

4. Clean Up Resources

After you finish using the TensorFlow Lite model, it is a good practice to release the interpreter resources.

```
override fun onDestroy() {
    super.onDestroy()
    tflite.close()
}
```

Integrating custom models with TensorFlow Lite into your Android application empowers you to provide advanced machine learning capabilities tailored to your specific needs. From preparing and converting your model to loading it in your app and running inference, this process enables you to harness the power of machine learning on mobile devices effectively. As you implement these features, keep in mind best practices for model optimization, input data preprocessing, and memory management to ensure your app remains responsive and efficient. By leveraging TensorFlow Lite, you can deliver intelligent applications that provide users with innovative and valuable experiences.

11.3 Optimizing Model Performance and Reducing Latency

Optimizing machine learning models for mobile devices is crucial for enhancing user experience, ensuring responsiveness, and managing resource consumption effectively. When integrating custom models using TensorFlow Lite (TFLite) in Android applications, it is important to focus on techniques that help reduce latency, decrease memory usage, and improve overall performance. This section will explore various strategies for optimizing model performance, including model quantization, optimizing input data, leveraging hardware acceleration, and using best practices in TFLite.

1. Model Quantization

Quantization is the process of reducing the precision of the numbers used to represent model parameters, which can lead to significant improvements in performance and reductions in model size. TFLite supports several types of quantization:

1.1 Post-Training Quantization

This method allows you to convert a trained model to a smaller size without the need for retraining. TFLite provides several quantization options:

Dynamic Range Quantization: Converts weights from float32 to int8 during inference, while keeping the activations in float32. This can reduce model size and improve speed, especially on devices with limited computational power.

converter.optimizations = [tf.lite.Optimize.DEFAULT]

Full Integer Quantization: This method quantizes both weights and activations to int8, which can further enhance performance on some hardware. It requires representative data to calibrate the quantization process.

converter.target_spec.supported_types = [tf.int8]

1.2 Quantization Aware Training (QAT)

For models that require higher accuracy after quantization, QAT simulates the effects of quantization during training. This technique helps the model learn to adapt to lower precision, leading to better performance when deployed.

import tensorflow_model_optimization as tfmot

 # Prepare your model with quantization aware layers
qat_model = tfmot.quantization.keras.quantize_annotate_model(original_model)
 # Fine-tune the model on your dataset

2. Optimize Input Data

The format and preprocessing of input data can significantly affect inference speed. Here are some strategies:

2.1 Input Resizing and Normalization

Ensure that input images are resized to the dimensions expected by the model before feeding them into the TFLite interpreter. Normalizing pixel values can also help in faster processing:

```
private fun prepareInput(image: Bitmap): Array<FloatArray> {
    val inputSize = 224 // Model's input size
    val resizedImage = Bitmap.createScaledBitmap(image, inputSize, inputSize, true)
    val inputArray = Array(1) { FloatArray(inputSize * inputSize * 3) }

    for (y in 0 until inputSize) {
      for (x in 0 until inputSize) {
        val pixel = resizedImage.getPixel(x, y)
        inputArray[0][y * inputSize + x] = Color.red(pixel) / 255.0f
        inputArray[0][y * inputSize + x + 1] = Color.green(pixel) / 255.0f
        inputArray[0][y * inputSize + x + 2] = Color.blue(pixel) / 255.0f
      }
    }
    return inputArray
}
```

2.2 Batch Processing

If your application processes multiple inputs (e.g., a batch of images), consider batching the inputs together to reduce overhead and maximize the use of the underlying hardware.

```
val inputArray = Array(batchSize) { FloatArray(inputSize * inputSize * 3) }
// Fill inputArray with batched data
tflite.run(inputArray, outputArray)
```

3. Hardware Acceleration

Utilizing hardware acceleration can lead to significant performance gains. TFLite supports several hardware acceleration options:

3.1 GPU Acceleration

Using GPU can speed up model inference significantly. To enable GPU support in TFLite, include the GPU delegate:

```
import org.tensorflow.lite.gpu.GpuDelegate

val options = Interpreter.Options().addDelegate(GpuDelegate())
val tflite = Interpreter(loadModelFile("model.tflite"), options)
```

3.2 NNAPI (Neural Networks API)

For Android devices, using NNAPI can take advantage of specialized hardware accelerators available on the device, improving performance for deep learning models. Use the NNAPI delegate when creating the interpreter:

```
import org.tensorflow.lite.nnapi.NnApiDelegate

val options = Interpreter.Options().addDelegate(NnApiDelegate())
val tflite = Interpreter(loadModelFile("model.tflite"), options)
```

4. Model Architecture Optimization

Optimizing the model architecture can also lead to better performance. Some strategies include:

4.1 Simplifying the Model

Reduce the complexity of the model by decreasing the number of layers or parameters, which can lead to faster inference times. Consider using lightweight architectures such as MobileNet, SqueezeNet, or EfficientNet.

4.2 Using Depthwise Separable Convolutions

For convolutional neural networks, replacing standard convolutions with depthwise separable convolutions can greatly reduce the number of parameters and computational load while maintaining accuracy.

```
model = tf.keras.Sequential([
    tf.keras.layers.Conv2D(32, (3, 3), padding='same', activation='relu',
input_shape=(img_height, img_width, 3)),
    tf.keras.layers.DepthwiseConv2D((3, 3), padding='same', activation='relu'),
    tf.keras.layers.GlobalAveragePooling2D(),
    tf.keras.layers.Dense(num_classes, activation='softmax')
])
```

5. Measuring and Monitoring Performance

To ensure your optimizations are effective, it is essential to measure and monitor the performance of your model in real-time.

5.1 Profiling Inference Time

You can measure the inference time of your model using System.nanoTime() before and after the inference call.

```
val startTime = System.nanoTime()
// Run the model
tflite.run(inputArray, outputArray)
val endTime = System.nanoTime()
val inferenceTime = (endTime - startTime) / 1_000_000 // Convert to milliseconds
Log.d("ModelPerformance", "Inference time: $inferenceTime ms")
```

5.2 Monitoring Resource Usage

Monitor CPU and memory usage while running the model to identify potential bottlenecks. Tools like Android Profiler in Android Studio can help analyze performance metrics and optimize resource consumption.

Optimizing machine learning models for mobile applications is essential for providing users with a seamless experience while maintaining efficient resource utilization. Techniques such as model quantization, optimizing input data, utilizing hardware acceleration, and refining model architecture can significantly enhance performance and reduce latency. By continuously measuring and monitoring model performance, you can identify areas for improvement and ensure that your application delivers fast, reliable, and intelligent features to users. With TensorFlow Lite, you have a robust framework to implement these optimizations effectively, making it easier to create high-performing machine learning applications on mobile devices.

Chapter 12: Testing, Debugging, and Performance Optimization

In this chapter, we will focus on the essential practices of testing, debugging, and optimizing the performance of your Android applications to ensure they run smoothly and reliably in real-world scenarios. You will learn how to implement unit tests and UI tests using frameworks like JUnit and Espresso, enabling you to validate your application's functionality and user interface effectively. We'll discuss strategies for writing effective tests, managing test cases, and using test doubles to isolate components for thorough testing. Additionally, we will cover debugging techniques, including using Android Studio's debugger, logging, and analyzing crash reports to identify and resolve issues efficiently. Performance optimization is crucial for providing a seamless user experience, so we will delve into profiling tools like Android Profiler to monitor memory usage, CPU activity, and network calls. You will also learn best practices for optimizing battery consumption and app responsiveness, ensuring that your application remains efficient under various conditions. By the end of this chapter, you will have the skills and knowledge to implement comprehensive testing and debugging strategies, as well as performance optimization techniques, to deliver high-quality, reliable Android applications that meet user expectations and stand out in the market.

12.1 Unit and UI Testing with JUnit and Espresso

Testing is an essential part of the software development lifecycle, ensuring that your application behaves as expected and provides a quality user experience. In Android development, two of the most widely used testing frameworks are JUnit for unit testing and Espresso for UI testing. This section will guide you through the processes of setting up, writing, and executing tests with JUnit and Espresso, as well as best practices to follow for effective testing.

1. Understanding the Testing Frameworks

1.1 JUnit

JUnit is a popular unit testing framework for Java applications, including Android. It provides annotations and assertions to facilitate the creation and execution of tests. Unit tests typically focus on individual components or methods, ensuring that they function correctly in isolation.

Key Features of JUnit:

- Annotations for test lifecycle management (e.g., @Test, @Before, @After).
- Assertions to verify expected outcomes (e.g., assertEquals, assertTrue).
- Test runners to execute tests and report results.

1.2 Espresso

Espresso is part of the Android Testing Support Library, designed specifically for UI testing. It provides a rich API to simulate user interactions and verify that the UI behaves as expected. Espresso allows developers to write concise and reliable tests for the user interface of their Android applications.

Key Features of Espresso:

- ViewMatchers to find UI components (e.g., onView(withId(R.id.button))).
- ViewActions to simulate user interactions (e.g., click(), typeText()).
- ViewAssertions to verify the state of UI components (e.g., check(matches(isDisplayed()))).

2. Setting Up the Testing Environment

To get started with testing in Android, ensure your project is correctly set up with the necessary dependencies.

2.1 Adding Dependencies

Open your build.gradle (Module: app) file and include the following dependencies:

```
dependencies {
    // JUnit for unit testing
    testImplementation 'junit:junit:4.13.2'

    // Espresso for UI testing
    androidTestImplementation 'androidx.test.espresso:espresso-core:3.5.1'
    androidTestImplementation 'androidx.test.ext:junit:1.1.5'
}
```

Sync your project to download the dependencies.

2.2 Organizing Test Directories

Android Studio automatically generates the necessary directories for tests:

- **Unit Tests**: Place your unit tests in the src/test/java/ directory.
- **UI Tests**: Place your UI tests in the src/androidTest/java/ directory.

3. Writing Unit Tests with JUnit

Unit tests focus on testing the logic of individual methods and classes.

3.1 Creating a Simple Unit Test

Create a new Java/Kotlin class in the src/test/java/ directory.

Use the @Test annotation to define a test method.

Example:

```
import org.junit.Assert.*
import org.junit.Test

class CalculatorTest {

    @Test
    fun addition_isCorrect() {
        val sum = add(2, 3)
        assertEquals(5, sum)
    }

    private fun add(a: Int, b: Int): Int {
        return a + b
    }
}
```

3.2 Running Unit Tests

- Right-click on the test class or method in Android Studio.
- Select Run 'CalculatorTest' to execute the tests.

- View the results in the Run window.

4. Writing UI Tests with Espresso

UI tests validate the interaction between the user and the application interface.

4.1 Creating a Simple UI Test

Create a new Java/Kotlin class in the src/androidTest/java/ directory.

Use the @RunWith(AndroidJUnit4::class) annotation to specify the test runner.

Example:

```
import androidx.test.ext.junit.runners.AndroidJUnit4
import androidx.test.rule.ActivityTestRule
import androidx.test.espresso.Espresso.onView
import androidx.test.espresso.action.ViewActions.click
import androidx.test.espresso.assertion.ViewAssertions.matches
import androidx.test.espresso.matcher.ViewMatchers.withId
import androidx.test.espresso.matcher.ViewMatchers.isDisplayed
import org.junit.Rule
import org.junit.Test
import org.junit.runner.RunWith

@RunWith(AndroidJUnit4::class)
class MainActivityTest {

    @get:Rule
    var activityRule = ActivityTestRule(MainActivity::class.java)

    @Test
    fun buttonClick_displaysToastMessage() {
        // Perform click action on the button
        onView(withId(R.id.my_button)).perform(click())

        // Verify that the toast message is displayed
        onView(withText("Button
clicked!")).inRoot(ToastMatcher()).check(matches(isDisplayed()))
    }
```

```
}
```

4.2 Creating a Custom Matcher for Toast Messages

Since toasts are not part of the view hierarchy, you need a custom matcher to verify their visibility:

```
import android.view.View
import android.widget.Toast
import androidx.test.espresso.matcher.BoundedMatcher
import org.hamcrest.Description
import org.hamcrest.Matcher

fun ToastMatcher(): Matcher<in View?> {
    return object : BoundedMatcher<View, Toast>(Toast::class.java) {
        override fun matchesSafely(toast: Toast): Boolean {
            return true // Customize logic as needed
        }

        override fun describeTo(description: Description) {
            description.appendText("is a toast")
        }
    }
}
```

5. Running UI Tests

- Right-click on the test class or method in Android Studio.
- Select Run 'MainActivityTest' to execute the tests.
- View the results in the Run window.

6. Best Practices for Testing

To maximize the effectiveness of your tests, consider the following best practices:

6.1 Keep Tests Isolated

Each test should be independent and not rely on the state or outcome of other tests. This ensures consistent results and easier debugging.

6.2 Use Meaningful Test Names

Name your test methods descriptively to indicate their purpose. This enhances readability and understanding of the test suite.

6.3 Test Edge Cases

Ensure that your tests cover various input scenarios, including edge cases. This helps identify potential issues that may not be apparent during normal operations.

6.4 Use Mocking for Dependencies

When testing classes with dependencies, use mocking frameworks like Mockito to simulate those dependencies. This helps isolate the unit being tested and avoids side effects.

testImplementation 'org.mockito:mockito-core:4.3.1'

Testing is a crucial aspect of Android development, and utilizing frameworks like JUnit for unit testing and Espresso for UI testing ensures that your application is robust and reliable. By following best practices, creating meaningful tests, and leveraging the features of these frameworks, you can significantly improve the quality of your codebase and enhance the user experience. With well-written tests, you can confidently make changes and additions to your code, knowing that you have mechanisms in place to catch regressions and ensure functionality.

12.2 Debugging Techniques and Crash Reporting

Debugging is an essential skill for developers, allowing them to identify and resolve issues in their applications effectively. In Android development, various tools and techniques can help you debug your applications, ensuring they run smoothly and reliably. Additionally, crash reporting is vital for maintaining application health, as it provides insights into runtime errors that may occur in production. This section will cover key debugging techniques, tools available in Android Studio, and effective strategies for implementing crash reporting.

1. Debugging Techniques

Debugging involves systematically identifying, isolating, and resolving bugs or issues in your code. Here are some key techniques to enhance your debugging process:

1.1 Log Statements

Using logging is one of the simplest yet most effective debugging techniques. By adding log statements throughout your code, you can trace the flow of execution and monitor variable values.

Using Logcat: Android provides a logging framework (android.util.Log) that allows you to output log messages to Logcat. Use different log levels (VERBOSE, DEBUG, INFO, WARN, ERROR, ASSERT) to categorize your log messages.

Example:

```
import android.util.Log

fun divide(a: Int, b: Int): Int {
    if (b == 0) {
        Log.e("Calculator", "Division by zero error")
        throw IllegalArgumentException("Cannot divide by zero")
    }
    Log.d("Calculator", "Dividing $a by $b")
    return a / b
}
```

Filtering Logcat: Use the Logcat window in Android Studio to filter logs by tag, log level, or keywords, making it easier to find relevant information.

1.2 Breakpoints

Setting breakpoints allows you to pause the execution of your application at a specific line of code, enabling you to inspect the current state of variables, the call stack, and more.

How to Set Breakpoints: Click on the gutter (left margin) next to the line number in Android Studio to set a breakpoint.

Running in Debug Mode: Run your application in debug mode (Shift + F9) to trigger the debugger. When the execution hits a breakpoint, you can inspect variable values and control the flow of execution.

Step Execution: Use step-in, step-over, and step-out features to navigate through your code while debugging. This allows you to observe how your application behaves line by line.

1.3 Inspecting Variables and the Call Stack

When your application is paused at a breakpoint, you can inspect variables and the call stack:

Variable Inspection: Hover over variables to see their current values, or use the Variables pane in the Debugger tool window.

Call Stack: The call stack shows the sequence of method calls that led to the current point of execution. It helps identify how your code reached a specific state.

2. Advanced Debugging Techniques

For more complex issues, consider these advanced debugging techniques:

2.1 Remote Debugging

Remote debugging allows you to connect to a device or emulator to debug an application running on it. This is particularly useful for testing on various Android versions and configurations.

Setting Up Remote Debugging: Connect your device via USB and enable USB debugging in Developer Options. Use adb commands to forward the debug port.

adb tcpip 5555
adb connect <device_ip_address>:5555

Attach Debugger: In Android Studio, use the "Attach Debugger" option to connect to the running application on the remote device.

2.2 Analyzing Memory Leaks

Memory leaks can lead to performance issues and application crashes. Use Android Profiler to monitor memory usage and identify leaks.

Memory Profiler: In Android Studio, navigate to View > Tool Windows > Profiler and select the Memory Profiler to analyze your app's memory allocation, identify leaks, and observe object retention.

LeakCanary: Consider integrating LeakCanary, an open-source library that automatically detects memory leaks in your application and provides helpful reports.

```
dependencies {
    debugImplementation 'com.squareup.leakcanary:leakcanary-android:2.7'
}
```

3. Crash Reporting

Despite best efforts in debugging, crashes can still occur in production. Implementing effective crash reporting helps developers understand and resolve issues quickly.

3.1 Using Firebase Crashlytics

Firebase Crashlytics is a powerful crash reporting tool that provides detailed insights into application crashes, including stack traces, device information, and user actions leading up to the crash.

Setting Up Firebase Crashlytics:

Add Firebase to Your Project: Go to the Firebase Console, create a new project, and follow the setup instructions to add Firebase SDK to your Android application.

Add Crashlytics Dependency:

```
dependencies {
    implementation 'com.google.firebase:firebase-crashlytics-ktx:18.2.6'
}
```

Initialize Crashlytics: Ensure that Crashlytics is initialized in your Application class or MainActivity.

```
class MyApplication : Application() {
    override fun onCreate() {
        super.onCreate()
        FirebaseApp.initializeApp(this)
```

```
    // Initialize Crashlytics
    FirebaseCrashlytics.getInstance().setCrashlyticsCollectionEnabled(true)
  }
}
```

Log Non-Fatal Errors: Use Crashlytics to log non-fatal exceptions or custom messages.

```
try {
    // Some risky operation
} catch (e: Exception) {
    FirebaseCrashlytics.getInstance().recordException(e)
}
```

Reviewing Crash Reports: In the Firebase Console, navigate to the Crashlytics dashboard to view crash reports, including stack traces and impacted users.

3.2 Other Crash Reporting Tools

While Firebase Crashlytics is a popular choice, there are other crash reporting tools available, such as:

- **Sentry**: Provides comprehensive error tracking and performance monitoring.
- **Rollbar**: Real-time error tracking with insights into how errors impact users.
- **Instabug**: Allows users to report bugs directly from the app with screenshots and logs.

4. Best Practices for Debugging and Crash Reporting

To maximize the effectiveness of your debugging and crash reporting strategies, consider the following best practices:

4.1 Write Comprehensive Test Cases

Ensure your application is thoroughly tested with unit tests and UI tests. This helps catch issues early in the development cycle, reducing the chances of runtime crashes.

4.2 Use Version Control

Implement version control (e.g., Git) to manage your codebase effectively. This allows you to track changes, revert to previous states, and collaborate with team members.

4.3 Analyze Crash Data Regularly

Regularly review crash reports to identify patterns or recurring issues. Prioritize fixing high-impact crashes that affect a significant number of users.

4.4 Monitor Application Performance

Use monitoring tools to track application performance metrics, such as CPU usage, memory consumption, and network latency. This helps identify performance bottlenecks that could lead to crashes.

Debugging and crash reporting are integral aspects of the Android development process, ensuring that applications function correctly and provide a seamless user experience. By employing effective debugging techniques, utilizing powerful tools like Android Studio and Firebase Crashlytics, and following best practices, developers can swiftly identify and resolve issues, ultimately delivering high-quality applications to users. With a proactive approach to debugging and crash reporting, you can enhance the stability and performance of your Android applications, fostering user satisfaction and retention.

12.3 Profiling for Memory, CPU, and Battery Optimization

Profiling is an essential practice in Android development that helps you analyze the performance of your application. By monitoring and optimizing memory usage, CPU consumption, and battery life, you can enhance the user experience and ensure that your app runs efficiently on various devices. This section explores the tools and techniques available for profiling Android applications, focusing on memory, CPU, and battery optimization.

1. Understanding Profiling

Profiling involves measuring various performance metrics of your application to identify areas that may need improvement. In Android, profiling can help you detect memory leaks, inefficient CPU usage, and excessive battery consumption, which are critical for maintaining the quality and performance of your app.

1.1 Why Profiling is Important

- **User Experience**: Apps that consume excessive resources can lead to lagging interfaces and slow response times, negatively impacting user satisfaction.
- **Device Performance**: Efficient resource management ensures that your app runs smoothly across different devices, especially those with limited hardware capabilities.
- **Battery Life**: Optimizing battery consumption is vital, as users prefer apps that do not drain their device's battery quickly.

2. Profiling Memory Usage

Memory profiling helps you track how your app utilizes memory and identify potential memory leaks. Android Studio provides several tools for monitoring memory usage:

2.1 Memory Profiler

Accessing Memory Profiler: In Android Studio, navigate to View > Tool Windows > Profiler. Connect your device or emulator, and select your app from the profiler window.

Analyzing Memory Usage:

- **Heap Dump**: Capture a heap dump to analyze memory allocation. This allows you to view the objects currently in memory, their references, and the overall memory footprint.
- **Allocation Tracking**: Monitor object allocations over time to identify which parts of your code consume the most memory.
- **Identifying Memory Leaks**: Use the Leak Canary library for automated leak detection. It provides insights when memory leaks occur and helps pinpoint the source.

```
dependencies {
    debugImplementation 'com.squareup.leakcanary:leakcanary-android:2.7'
}
```

2.2 Using Allocation Tracker

The Allocation Tracker in Android Studio helps visualize memory usage over time, allowing you to spot spikes in memory consumption.

- **Start Tracking**: Click on the "Record Allocations" button to start tracking memory allocations.

- **Analyze**: Review the recorded data to see which objects were allocated, how long they lived, and their reference paths.

3. Profiling CPU Usage

Profiling CPU usage is crucial for identifying performance bottlenecks and ensuring your application runs efficiently.

3.1 CPU Profiler

Accessing CPU Profiler: From the Profiler window, select the CPU option. You can record the CPU usage while your application runs.

Analyzing CPU Usage:

- **Method Tracing**: This tool records method calls and displays the time spent in each method. It helps identify slow methods and areas for optimization.
- **Thread Monitoring**: Observe the behavior of different threads in your application, checking for idle time, CPU usage, and potential deadlocks.

Understanding CPU Usage Metrics:

- **Total CPU Usage**: Displays the overall CPU usage of your application.
- **Thread Activity**: Shows the active threads and the CPU time consumed by each.

3.2 Optimizing CPU Usage

- **Profile-Driven Development**: Use the profiler data to refactor inefficient code. For example, avoid long-running tasks on the main thread to prevent UI freezes.
- **Use Background Threads**: Offload intensive tasks to background threads using AsyncTask, Thread, or Executors to keep the UI responsive.

4. Profiling Battery Consumption

Battery optimization is crucial for user satisfaction. Excessive battery drain can lead to app uninstalls or negative reviews.

4.1 Battery Historian

Battery Historian is a powerful tool for analyzing battery consumption in Android applications.

- Generating Battery Reports:
- Connect your device and run your application for a while to gather usage data.

Use adb to generate a battery report:

adb shell dumpsys batterystats > battery_stats.txt

Analyzing Battery Stats:

- Open the Battery Historian tool (usually a web-based interface) to visualize the report.
- Identify the components consuming the most battery power and the time spent in various states (e.g., idle, active).

4.2 Android Profiler Battery Stats

The Android Profiler also provides battery usage stats:

Accessing Battery Profiler: From the Profiler window, click on the Battery tab to view battery consumption metrics.

Key Metrics:

- **Wake Locks**: Track wake locks held by your application, which can lead to battery drain.
- **Network Activity**: Monitor network requests, as they can significantly impact battery life.

4.3 Implementing Battery Optimization Techniques

- **Use JobScheduler or WorkManager**: Schedule background tasks to run when the device is idle or connected to a power source.
- **Optimize Network Usage**: Minimize network requests and consider using batch requests to reduce power consumption.
- **Use Efficient Algorithms**: Ensure that the algorithms you use are optimized for performance and resource usage.

5. General Optimization Best Practices

To ensure optimal performance in your Android applications, adhere to these general best practices:

5.1 Optimize Layouts

- **Flatten View Hierarchies**: Reduce the number of nested views in your layout to improve rendering performance.
- **Use ConstraintLayout**: Utilize ConstraintLayout for creating complex layouts while maintaining flat hierarchies.

5.2 Reduce Resource Size

- **Optimize Bitmaps**: Use scaled-down versions of images and avoid using large images unnecessarily.
- **Use Vector Drawables**: Opt for vector graphics where possible, as they are resolution-independent and often smaller in size.

5.3 Monitor Performance Continuously

- **Integrate Performance Monitoring Tools**: Consider using tools like Firebase Performance Monitoring to continuously monitor your app's performance in production.

Profiling your Android application for memory, CPU, and battery optimization is essential for delivering a smooth user experience and maintaining performance across devices. By utilizing the various profiling tools available in Android Studio and adhering to best practices, you can effectively identify bottlenecks, optimize resource usage, and ensure that your app runs efficiently. Regular profiling and optimization should be part of your development cycle, helping to maintain high-quality applications that meet user expectations. With careful attention to performance, you can create applications that are not only functional but also enjoyable for users to interact with, fostering engagement and retention.

Advanced Android Programming: Harnessing the Power of Mobile Apps is an essential guide for experienced developers looking to master the intricacies of Android development. Authored by Alexeyzz Kuznetsov, a seasoned mobile app developer and software architect, this book goes beyond foundational skills to cover advanced topics and cutting-edge techniques that elevate Android applications to new heights of performance, functionality, and user engagement.

This book dives into Android's complex architecture, efficient UI design with Jetpack Compose, and sophisticated navigation strategies, helping developers create modular, maintainable, and visually dynamic apps. From data management with Room and ViewModel to networking with Retrofit, dependency injection with Dagger and Hilt, and background processing with Coroutines and WorkManager, Advanced Android Programming equips readers with the tools needed to develop robust applications that perform seamlessly in real-world conditions.

For developers keen on expanding their knowledge further, this book explores high-demand areas like machine learning integration using TensorFlow Lite, enhancing user experiences with animations and transitions, building secure applications, and optimizing app performance. Each chapter is crafted with practical insights, best practices, and code examples, providing hands-on knowledge that translates directly into professional app development.

Whether you're a developer aiming to build sophisticated, high-quality Android apps or a tech enthusiast eager to push the boundaries of mobile capabilities, Advanced Android Programming: Harnessing the Power of Mobile Apps is your comprehensive roadmap to success in Android development.